wagner im festspielhaus

*discography of the
bayreuth recordings
compiled by john hunt*

RICHARD WAGNER
BAYREUTH FESTIVAL, 1927
COLUMBIA RECORDS

Issued with the Approval of
Siegfried Wagner, Bayreuth

Wagner im Festspielhaus: an introduction

Everything surrounding the personality of Richard Wagner is of necessity on a broad and generous scale. Starting with the music dramas themselves, this also embraces the writings both philosophical and autobiographical, the business activities leading to the construction of Bayreuth, and not least to the promotion of his own image. Had Wagner been active in an era such as ours, with its dependance on highly sophisticated media, we can be sure that he would have made full use of radio, film and internet. Indeed the music dramas might well have been conceived for television instead of having to wait, as they did, for the development of the gramophone before they could reach the massive audiences which the composer had in mind.

Official Wagner editions, comprising authorised recordings made in the Festspielhaus either with or without audience and capturing the essential acoustic characteristic of the house, have been suprisingly few. Between 1927 and 1936 Columbia and Telefunken were allowed to record there, using the singers who had been engaged for the stage performances. After the 1951 re-opening both Columbia and Decca were active in setting down entire works, or entire acts, for the newly introduced long playing records, but it appears that problems of both contractual and technical natures brought these particular activities to a close by 1956.

Philips was the next record label to participate, having by the 1980s built up a catalogue of live performances in sound and on film which they eventually introduced as their *Wagner- Edition*, comprising all the mature works which Cosima Wagner had deemed worthy of performance at Bayreuth. These are the works which to this day have constituted the repertory of the annual Bayreuth Festival. All the recordings mentioned so far were made without an audience present or edited from a mixture of rehearsal and actual public performance, or, in the case of versions for film (video cassette, laserdisc, dvd video), specially performed and recorded either just before or after the actual Festival period of July-August each year.

Finally, during the last three years Festival chief Wolfgang Wagner has begun authorising an edition of post-war stage performances from the Festival, officially edited as representing the very best of Bayreuth's achievement: so far *Tristan und Isolde* (Karajan 1952), *Tannhäuser* (Cluytens 1955) and *Der Ring des Nibelungen* (Knappertsbusch 1956) have appeared on the Orfeo label.

DEN FREUNDEN RICHARD WAGNERS
präsentiert
PHILIPS
Originalaufnahmen der Bayreuther Festspiele 1961 und 1962
in Gesamtausgaben.
Kassetten mit reich illustrierten Textbeilagen.

PARSIFAL
Musikalische Leitung: Hans Knappertsbusch

Kundry .... Irene Dalis	Parsifal .... Jess Thomas
Amfortas ..... George London	Gurnemanz ..... Hans Hotter
Titurel .... Martti Talvela	Klingsor .... Gustav Neidlinger

Niels Möller · Gerd Nienstedt · Sona Cervena · Ursula Boese
Gerhard Stolze · Georg Paskuda · Gundula Janowitz · Anja Silja
Else-Margrete Gardelli · Dorothea Siebert · Rita Bartos

A 02 342/346 L mono · 835 220/224 AY stereo
Subskriptionspreis DM 90,—
ab 1.1.1965   DM 125,—

TANNHÄUSER
Musikalische Leitung: Wolfgang Sawallisch

Elisabeth .... Anja Silja	Wolfram ... Eberhard Wächter
Venus .... Grace Bumbry	Walther ..... Gerhard Stolze
Tannhäuser .. Wolfg. Windgassen	Biterolf .... Franz Crass
Landgraf ...... Josef Greindl	Heinrich der Schreiber G. Paskuda

Gerd Nienstedt · Else-Margrete Gardelli

A 02 303/05 L mono · 835 178/80 AY stereo · DM 75,—

DER FLIEGENDE HOLLÄNDER
Musikalische Leitung: Wolfgang Sawallisch

Senta .... Anja Silja	Daland .... Josef Greindl
Mary .... Res Fischer	Erik .... Fritz Uhl
Holländer ...... Franz Crass	Steuermann ... Georg Paskuda

A 02 211/13 L mono · 835 104/06 AY stereo · DM 75,—

Chor und Orchester der Bayreuther Festspiele
Chordirektor: Wilhelm Pitz
Regie und Inszenierung: Wieland Wagner

ungeb. Preise

However, this is by far from the entire story. An article in a festival programme book from the early 1980s asserted that live radio transmissions of individual acts started taking place immediately when the Bayreuth Festival re-opened after World War I (1924), although it seems unlikely that any of these would have been preserved or even relayed to other countries. However, starting tentatively in 1931, then continuing during the years of the Third Reich and proceeding with force from 1951, live radio transmissions of Bayreuth performances became the norm, recorded by *Bayerischer Rundfunk* but sold on to other German radio stations as well as all over Europe and beyond. These were naturally recorded and preserved by collectors both professional and amateur, a fact which must have been recognised in the fees charged by Bayreuth for allowing the performances to be disseminated in this way. It was then inevitable, when so-called pirate LPs began to circulate on a large scale around the early 1970s, that Bayreuth's legacy would form an important part of the vast but albeit unofficial treasure trove available to opera lovers across the entire world – all this regardless of whether the Bayreuth Festival authorities considered it desirable or otherwise.

Even before the Columbia sessions in 1927, soon after the introduction of electrical recording made reproduction of a full symphony orchestra a feasible proposition, pioneer Fred Gaisberg had been in Bayreuth as early as 1904 with his portable recording equipment in order to record artists who were participating in that year's festival. These sessions did not take place in the *Festspielhaus* but in *Hotel Sonne*, situated quite near Villa Wahnfried on the Richard-Wagner-Strasse (that hotel building is long since demolished). They are included in the discography as an integral part of Bayreuth's aural history, even when the singers are performing music not composed by Wagner. We are also told that much more material was recorded in 1904 than was actually published, although many discerning connoisseurs may deem that to be a blessing, considering the variable quality of the singing on those one-sided discs.

Likewise in more modern times, recorded visits by Bayreuth forces to Europe and beyond (Barcelona 1955, Japan 1967 and 1989) can also be considered to be part of the legacy documented here – even if other orchestras may have been employed on occasion.

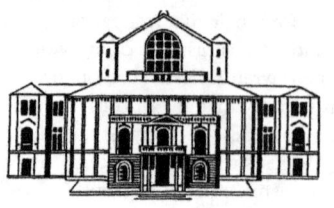

Die festliche Bayreuther Atmosphäre in Ihrem Heim

DURCH BAYREUTHER ORIGINAL-AUFNAHMEN

LOHENGRIN	LXT-2880-84
DER FLIEGENDE HOLLÄNDER	LXT-5150-52
PARSIFAL	LXT-2651-56

MIT DEN DIRIGENTEN
JOSEPH KEILBERTH UND HANS KNAPPERTSBUSCH
UND DEN SOLISTEN
JOSEF GREINDL · GEORG LONDON · MARTHA MÖDL
ASTRID VARNAY · WOLFGANG WINDGASSEN
AUSSCHLIESSLICH AUF DECCA-LANGSPIELPLATTEN

WEITERE 50 VOLLSTÄNDIGE OPERNAUFNAHMEN IM FÜHRENDEN KLASSISCHEN DECCA-REPERTOIRE SIND EIN EINMALIGES DOKUMENT INTERNATIONALER OPERNTRADITION.

SONDER-PROSPEKTE ERHALTEN SIE BEI IHREM SCHALLPLATTEN-FACHHÄNDLER

TELEFUNKEN

DECCA

RCA

TELDEC »TELEFUNKEN-DECCA« SCHALLPLATTEN G.M.B.H.

A tradition inaugurated by Wagner himself when the foundation stone of the *Festspielhaus* was laid in 1872 was the playing of Beethoven's Ninth Symphony. This was continued intermittently by Richard Strauss in 1933 (on the fiftieth anniversary of Wagner's death), by Wilhelm Furtwängler in 1951 and 1954, by Paul Hindemith in 1953, by Karl Böhm in 1963 and, most recently, by Christian Thielemann in 2001 (marking both 125 years since the opening of the Bayreuth Festival and 50 years since the post-war re-opening). Where recordings exist, these are also included in the discography, as are various commemorative concerts in 1966 (on the death of Wieland Wagner), 1983 (on the centenary of Richard Wagner's death), 1986 (on the centenary of Franz Liszt's death) and in 2005 (in honour of Cosima, Siegfried and Winifred Wagner).

Sources which I have referred to are Bayreuth Festival almanachs and individual programme books, *Wagners Werk und Wirkung* (Ellwanger-Verlag Bayreuth 1983 – giving complete cast lists from 1876 until 1983), *Parsifal on Record* by Jonathan Brown (Greenwood Press 1992), *Tristan on Record* by Jonathan Brown (Greenwood Press 2000) and the German radio periodical *Hör Zu*, a complete run of which, from 1951 until 2004, was made available to me by the library service of Berlin's *Freie Universität*. The catalogue accompanying a 2004 exhibition organised by the *Richard-Wagner-Museum* and entitled *Ton-Spuren: 100 Jahre Bayreuther Festspiele auf Schallplatte* was interesting, but almost completely ignored the wealth of existing live material. Individuals who have assisted my research include Yasushi Aisa, Mike Ashman (among other things he kindly made available to me data which he had obtained from *Bayerischer Rundfunk*), John Baker, the late David Crighton, Dennis Davis, John Hancock, Klaus Heinze, Bill Holland, Roderick Krüsemann, Sigrid Leonhardt, Ernst Lumpe, Luis Luna, Aman Pedersen and Malcolm Walker.

As already stated, radio broadcasts beginning in 1951 originated from *Bayerischer Rundfunk* but were invariably taken up by the other principal German stations (*Sender Freies Berlin, Norddeutscher Rundfunk, Westdeutscher Rundfunk, Hessischer Rundfunk* and so on), so that it is not always possible to pinpoint the source of circulating tapes. Of the various unofficial publications of these broadcasts, pride of place must go to the LP issues of the 1980s on the *Melodram* label, master-minded by the late Jürgen Grundheber, and on

CD to *Archipel/Gebhardt* with a series which promises to become a comprehensive survey of all the post-war broadcasts. Details of the publications in recent years described as from a private edition in vienna can be requested from the e-mail address amanp@utanet.at

Notwithstanding the complexity of the task, a simple one-column layout has been adopted. Performances or groups of excerpts are listed by number and date; conductors and all-important chorus-masters are named first, then followed by catalogue numbers of known issues, and finally (in a smaller type size) the casts for each performance.

Wagner Im Festspielhaus
Published by John Hunt.
© 2006 John Hunt
reprinted 2009
ISBN 978-1-901395-20-4

Sole distributors:
Travis & Emery,
17 Cecil Court,
London, WC2N 4EZ,
United Kingdom.
(+44) 20 7 459 2129.
sales@travis-and-emery.com

1 / 23-31 july 1904
recordings made by gramophone and typewriter company in hotel sonne, richard-wagner-strasse

tannhäuser: dir töne lob!
gramophone 2-42924
lp: emi 1C181 30669-30678M

desider matray (tannhäuser)
bruno seidler-winkler (piano accompaniment)

tannhäuser: frau holda kam aus dem berg hervor
gramophone 43576
lp: emi 1C181 30669-30678M
cd: gebhardt JGCD 0062

gertrude foerstel (ein junger hirt)
cor anglais accompaniment

tannhäuser: dich treff ich hier in dieser halle
gramophone 042083
cd: gebhardt JGCD 0062

katharina fleischer-edel (elisabeth)
paul knüpfer (landgraf)
bruno seidler-winkler (piano accompaniment)

tannhäuser heraus zum kampfe mit uns allen!
gramophone 2-42916
lp: emi 1C181 30669-30678M
cd: gebhardt JGCD 0062

robert von scheidt (biterolf)
bruno seidler-winkler (piano accompaniment)

tannhäuser: wohl wusst' ich hier sie im gebet zu finden
gramophone 2-42921
cd: symposium 1081
cd: gebhardt JGCD 0062

clarence whitehill (wolfram)
bruno seidler-winkler (piano accompaniment)

23-31 july 1904/continued
das rheingold: wallala! wallala!
gramophone 44406
lp: emi 1C181 30669-30678M
cd: gebhardt JGCD 0062

josephine von artner (woglinde)
marie knüpfer-egli (wellgunde)
ottilie metzger (flosshilde)
bruno seidler-winkler (piano accompaniment)

das rheingold: sanft schloss dein aug
gramophone 2-42918
lp: emi 1C181 30669-30678M
cd: gebhardt JGCD 0062

leon rains (wotan and fasolt)
bruno seidler-winkler (piano accompaniment)

das rheingold: wer hälfe mir? gehorchen muss ich (mimes erzählung)
gramophone 2-42922
lp: emi 1C181 30669-30678M
cd: symposium 1081
cd: gebhardt JGCD 0062

hans breuer (mime)
otto briesemeister (loge)
bruno seidler-winkler (piano accompaniment)

das rheingold: die in linder lüfte weh'n
gramophone 2-42919
lp: emi 1C181 30669-30678M
cd: gebhardt JGCD 0062

robert von scheidt (alberich)
bruno seidler-winkler (piano accompaniment)

23-31 july 1904/continued
das rheingold: abendlich strahlt der sonne auge
gramophone 2-42917
lp: emi 1C181 30669-30678M
cd: symposium 1081
cd: gebhardt JGCD 0062

theodor bertram (wotan)
bruno seidler-winkler (piano accompaniment)

das rheingold: so weit leben und weben (loges erzählung)
gramophone 2-42920
cd: symposium 1081
cd: gebhardt JGCD 0062

otto briesemeister (loge)
bruno seidler-winkler (piano accompaniment)

die walküre: winterstürme wichen dem wonnemond
gramophone 2-42925
cd: symposium 1081
cd: gebhardt JGCD 0062

alfred von bary (siegmund)
bruno seidler-winkler (piano accompaniment)

die walküre: siegmund heiss ich und siegmund bin ich!
gramophone 2-42926
lp: emi 1C181 30669-30678M
cd: symposium 1081
cd: gebhardt JGCD 0062

alfred von bary (siegmund)
bruno seidler-winkler (piano accompaniment)

siegfried: das ist nun der liebe schlimmer lohn/als zullendes kind
gramophone 2-42923
lp: emi 1C181 30669-30678M
cd: symposium 1081
cd: gebhardt JGCD 0062

hans breuer (mime)
bruno seidler-winkler (piano accompaniment)

14
23-31 july 1904/continued
siegfried: hei! siegfried gehört nun der niblungen hort
gramophone 43575
lp: emi 1C181 30669-30678M
cd: symposium 1081
cd: gebhardt JGCD 0062

emilie feuge-gleiss (waldvogel)
bruno seidler-winkler (piano accompamiment)

götterdämmerung: frau sonne sendet lichte strahlen
gramophone 44297
lp: emi 1C181 30669-30678M
cd: gebhardt JGCD 0062

josephine von artner (woglinde)
marie knüpfer-egli (wellgunde)
ottilie metzger (flosshilde)
bruno seidler-winkler (piano accompaniment)

mozart le nozze di figaro: non so piu *sung in german*
gramophone 43578
cd: gebhardt JGCD 0062

josephine von artner (cherubino)
bruno seidler-winkler (piano accompaniment)

flotow alessandro stradella: seid meiner wonne stille zeugen
gramophone 043043
cd: gebhardt JGCD 0062

emilie feuge-gleiss (leonora)
bruno seidler-winkler (piano accompaniment)

bizet carmen: pres des remparts de séville *sung in german*
gramophone 43585
cd: gebhardt JGCD 0062

ottile metzger (carmen)
bruno seidler-winkler (piano accompaniment)

23-31 july 1904/concluded
abt: wenn man beim wein sitzt
gramophone 2-42942
cd: gebhardt JGCD 0062

julius von scheidt (belamy)
robert von scheidt (bauer)
bruno seidler-winkler (piano accompaniment)

traditional: ui das tut guat
gramophone 44407
cd: gebhardt JGCD 0062

selma von scheidt
julius von scheidt
bruno seidler-winkler (piano accompaniment)

leoncavallo i pagliacci: e allor perché tu m'hai stregato *sung in german*
gramophone 44299
cd: gebhardt JGCD 0062

selma von scheidt (nedda)
julius von scheidt (silvio)
bruno seidler-winkler (piano accompaniment)

viellunger: zillertal du bist mei freud'!
gramophone 44401
cd: gebhardt JGCD 0062

selma von scheidt
julius von scheidt
bruno seidler-winkler (piano accompaniment)

16
2/august 1927
recordings made without audience by the columbia graphophone company

parsifal: verwandlungsmusik act one
bayreuth festival orchestra
conductor karl muck

78: columbia L 2007
78: columbia (germany) CLX 12515
78: columbia (usa) 67364D
lp: columbia (italy) QCX 10464
lp: melodiya M10 42887-42888
lp: pearl OPAL 837-838
cd: pearl GEMMCD 9843
cd: preiser 90393
cd: gebhardt JGCD 0063
cd: malibran CDRG 134
cd: naxos 811.0049-0050

august 1927/concluded
parsifal: zum letzten liebesmahle (gralsszene)
bayreuth festival orchestra and chorus
conductor karl muck
chorus-master hugo rüdel

78: columbia L 2008-2010
78: columbia (germany) CLX 12516-12518
78: columbia (usa) 67365D-67367D
lp: columbia (italy) QCX 10464
lp: emi 1C049 30679M/1C137 78174-78175M/1C181 30669-30678M
lp: melodiya M10 42887-42888
lp: discocorp IGI 379
lp: pearl OPAL 837-838
cd: pearl GEMMCD 9843
cd: preiser 90393
cd: naxos 811.0049-0050
1C049 30679M and 1C181 30669-30678M contained only the first part of the scene;
IGI 379 incorrectly described the recording as a live performance from the 1930s

parsifal: komm holder knabe! (blumenmädchenszene)
bayreuth festival orchestra
conductor karl muck

78: columbia L 2011
78: columbia (germany) CLX 12519
78: columbia (usa) 67368D
lp: columbia (italy) QCX 10464
lp: electrola E 83387
lp: emi 1C137 78174-78175M/1C181 30669-30678M
lp: melodiya M10 42887-42888
lp: pearl OPAL 837-838
cd: pearl GEMMCD 9843
cd: preiser 90393
cd: malibran CDRG 134
cd: naxos 811.0049-0050

fritz wolff (parsifal)
ingeborg holmgren (1.blumenmädchen)
anny helm (2.blumenmädchen)
minni ruske-leopold (3.blumenmädchen)
hilde sinnek (4.blumenmädchen)
maria nezadal (5.blumenmädchen)
chatlotte müller (6.blumenmädchen)

3/**18 august 1927**
recordings made without audience by the columbia graphophone company

parsifal: prelude act three
bayreuth festival orchestra
conductor siegfried wagner

78: columbia L 2012
78: columbia (germany) CLX 12520
78: columbia (usa) 67369D
lp: columbia (italy) QCX 10464
lp: emi 1C137 78174-78175M/1C147 30647-30648M
lp: trax classique TRXLP 112
cd: trax classique TRXCD 112
cd: preiser 90393
cd: malibran CDRG 134

parsifal: so ward es uns verhiessen (karfeitagszauber)
bayreuth festival orchestra
conductor siegfried wagner

78: columbia L 2013-2014
78: columbia (germany) CLX 12521-12522
78: columbia 67370D-67371D
lp: columbia (italy) QCX 10464
lp: electrola E 83387
lp: emi 1C137 78174-78175M/1C147 30647-30648M/1C181 30669-30678M/
    EX 29 02123
lp: angel seraphim 60124
lp: rca MET 404
lp: discocorp IGI 379
lp: trax classique TRXLP 112
cd: trax classique TRXCD 112
cd: musica memoria MM 30285
cd: preiser 90393
MET 404 contained only part three of the scene; IGI 379 incorrectly described the recording as a 1933 live performance conducted by richard strauss

fritz wolff (parsifal)
alexander kipnis (gurnemanz)

4/august 1927
recordings made without audience by the columbia graphophone company

das rheingold: einzug der götter/gesang der rheintöchter
bayreuth festival orchestra
conductor franz von hoesslin

78: columbia L 2016/LCX 45
78: columbia (germany) CLX 12524
78: columbia (italy) GQX 10482
78: columbia (usa) M 338
78: columbia (argentina) 266125
cd: preiser 90393
cd: malibran CDRG 134

maria nezadal (woglunde)
minni ruske-leopold (wellgunde)
charlotte müller (flosshilde)

die walküre: walkürenritt
bayreuth festival orchestra
conductor franz von hoesslin

78: columbia L 2017
78: columbia (germany) CLX 12525
78: columbia (usa) M 338
78: columbia (argentina) 264698
cd: preiser 90393
cd: malibran CDRG 134

ingeborg holmgren (gerhilde)
maria nezadal (ortlinde)
henriette gottlieb (waltraute)
elli sendler (schwertleite)
minni ruske-leopold (helmwige)
charlotte rückforth (siegrune)
charlotte müller (rossweisse)
maria peschken (grimgerde)

august 1927/concluded
siegfried: waldweben (forest murmurs)
bayreuth festival orchestra
conductor franz von hoesslin

78: columbia L 2014/LCX 43
78: columbia (germany) CLX 12522
78: columbia (usa) M 337
cd: preiser 90393
cd: malibran CDRG 134

siegfried: prelude to act three
bayreuth festival orchestra
conductor franz von hoesslin

78: columbia LCX 44
78: columbia (germany) CLX 12523
cd: preiser 90393
cd: malibran CDRG 134

siegfried: fire music (siegfried approaches brünnhilde's rock)
bayreuth festival orchestra
conductor franz von hoesslin

78: columbia L 2015/LCX 44
78: columbia (germany) CLX 12523
78: columbia (usa) M 338
78: columbia (argentina) 264699
cd: preiser 90393
cd: malibran CDRG 134

5/july 1928
recording made without audience by the columbia graphophone company

tristan und isolde *abridged version*
bayreuth festival orchestra and chorus
conductor karl elmendorff
chorus-master hugo rüdel

78: columbia L 2187-2206/LCX 64-83
78: columbia (germany) DWX 1273-1291
78: columbia (usa) M 101/OP 23
lp: columbia (usa) EL 11
lp: emi 1C181 03031-03033M
cd: malibran CDRG 102
cd: grammofono AB 78925-78926
cd: arkadia 78052
cd: preiser 90383
cd: naxos 811.0200-0202
excerpts
lp: electrola E 83387/WCLP 819
lp: emi 1C049 30679M/1C181 30669-30678M/EX 29 02123
lp: preiser LV 174
lp: bluebell B 196
cd: emi CMS 764 0082
cd: victoire 290.252
cd: preiser 89121/89986
L 2187-2206 and LCX 64-83 included two sides on which ernest newman (english version) and m.schneider and m.bérard (french version) explained the leitmotifs and their function: the english version of this is included on the naxos cd re-issue

nanny larsen-todsen (isolde)
anny helm (brangäne)
gunnar graarud (tristan)
rudolf bockelmann (kurwenal)
ivar andresen (marke)
joachim sattler (melot)
hanns beer (hirt)
gustav rödin (ein junger seemann)

22
6 / **july-august 1930**
recording made without audience by the columbia graphophone company

tannhäuser
abridged for recording purposes under the supervision of ernest newman and siegfried wagner
bayreuth festival orchestra and chorus
conductor karl elmendorff
chorus-master hugo rüdel

78: columbia LX 81-98/LCX 46-63
78: columbia (germany) LWX 3310-3327
78: columbia (france) LFX 112-129
78: columbia (argentina) 266414-266431
78: columbia (usa) M 151/OP 24
lp: emi 1C137 03130-03132M
cd: pearl GEMMCD 9941
cd: malibran CDRG 113
cd: naxos 811.0094-0095
excerpts
78: columbia (germany) LWX 88-95
78: columbia (canada) 9131M
lp: electrola E 83387
lp: emi RLS 7711/1C137 54390-54396M
cd: preiser 89235
according to ward marston in the notes to the naxos edition the landgrave's address (ein furchtbares verbrechen ward hier begangen) is taken from another recording of the piece by ivar andresen; stage performances of tannhäuser at the 1930 festival were conducted by arturo toscanini

maria müller (elisabeth)
ruth jost-arden (venus)
erna berger (ein junger hirt)
sigismund pilinsky (tannhäuser)
geza belti-pilinsky (walther von der vogelweide)
joachim sattler (heinrich der schreiber)
georg von tschurtschenthaler (biterolf)
herbert janssen (wolfram von eschenbach)
ivar andresen (landgraf)
carl stralendorf (reinmar von zweter)

7/18 august 1931
fragments recorded from the first european radio transmission of a bayreuth festival performance

tristan und isolde: ein siecher mann elend im sterben lag....das schwert ich liess es fallen
bayreuth festival orchestra
conductor wilhelm furtwängler

lp: danacord DACO 131-133
cd: istituto discografico italiano IDIS 330-331

nanny larsen-todsen (isolde)
anny helm (brangäne)

tristan und isolde: so reihte sie die mutter.....ans land ihn zu begleiten
bayreuth festival orchestra
conductor wilhelm furtwängler

lp: danacord DACO 131-133
cd: istituto discografico italiano IDIS 330-331

nanny larsen-todsen (isolde)
anny helm (brangäne)
rudolf bockelmann (kurwenal)

tristan und isolde: müht euch die?.....dass du nicht dir's entfallen lässt
bayreuth festival orchestra
conductor wilhelm furtwängler

lp: danacord DACO 131-133
cd: istituto discografico italiano IDIS 330-331

nanny larsen-todsen (isolde)
gotthelf pistor (tristan)

recording of the tristan prelude published on various unofficial labels as being from this performance was actually furtwängler's 1938 hmv studio version; however 1931 version of the prelude did exist in the deutsches rundfunkarchiv, according to research by mike ashman

24
8 / august 1933
reichsrundfunk broadcast

parsifal
bayreuth festival orchestra and chorus
conductor richard strauss
chorus-master hugo rüdel

max lorenz (parsifal)
marta fuchs (kundry)
heinrich schlusnus (amfortas)
alexander kipnis (gurnemanz)
gotthold ditter (klingsor)
ivar andresen (titurel)
enid szantho (stimme von oben & 1.knappe)
fritz marcks (1.gralsritter)
hans wrana (2.gralsritter)
irmingard scheidemantel (2.knappe & 5.blumenmädchen)
edwin heyer (3.knappe)
gerhard witting (4.knappe)
marcelle bunlet (1.blumenmädchen)
irene hoebink (2.blumenmädchen)
hildegard weigel (3.blumenmädchen)
emy von stetten (4.blumenmädchen)
margery booth (6.blumenmädchen)

according to research carried out by mike ashman, prelude and karfreiragszauber (szene des gurnemanz) did exist in deutsches rundfunkarchiv; however excerpts published on lp by discocorp and acanta (and most recently on cd by archipel ARPCD 0186) seem unlikely to be taken from this performance

9/4 august 1933
reichsrundfunk broadcast of performance marking fiftieth anniversary of wagner's death
beethoven: symphony no 9 "choral"

bayreuth festival orchestra and chorus
conductor richard strauss
chorus-master hugo rüdel

lilly neitzer
kirsten flagstad
fritz wolff
rudolf bockelmann

according to research by mike ashman, fragments from the second, third and fourth movements
existed in deutsches rundfunkarchiv

10/6 august 1933
reichsrundfunk broadcast

die meistersinger von nürnberg
bayreuth festival orchestra and chorus
conductor karl elmendorff
chorus-master hugo rüdel

käthe heidersbach (eva)
ruth berglund (magdalene)
max lorenz (stolzing)
erich zimmermann (david)
rudolf bockelmann (sachs)
alexander kipnis (pogner)
robert burg (kothner)
eugen fuchs (beckmesser)
willy störring (vogelgesang)
hans wrana (nachtigall)
gerhard witting (zorn)
harry steier (eisslinger)
fritz marcks (moser)
edwin heyer (ortel)
franz sauer (schwarz)
richard ludewigs (foltz)
fritz brauer (nachtwächter)

according to research by mike ashman, extensive excerpts from the performance
existed in deutsches rundfunkarchiv

11/**july 1934**
newsreel film fragment from a rehearsal performance

götterdämmerung: zu neuen taten teurer helde!
bayreuth festival orchestra
conductor karl elmendorff

frida leider (brünnhilde)
max lorenz (siegfried)

this extract has been shown in numerous film documentaries on wagner and bayreuth

12/**6 august 1934**
reichsrundfunk broadcast

die walküre
bayreuth festival orchestra
conductor karl elmendorff

unpublished reichsrundfunk recording
fragments from act three
lp: ed smith UORC 264

frida leider (brünnhilde)
maria müller (sieglinde)
sigrid onegin (fricka)
franz völker (siegmund)
rudolf bockelmann (wotan)
josef von manowards (hunding)
melitta amerling (gerhilde)
erna aubel (ortlinde)
carin carlsson (waltraute)
lilly neitzer (schwertleite)
grete kraiger (helmwige)
margery booth (siegrune)
rut berglund (grimgerde)
hanna kerrl (rossweisse)

according to research by mike ashman, the complete first act from this recording existed in deutsches rundfunkarchiv

13/**8 august 1934**
reichsrundfunk broadcast

siegfried
bayreuth festival orchestra
conductor karl elmendorff

unpublished reichsrundfunk recording

frida leider (brünnhilde)
käthe heidersbach (waldvogel)
sigrid onegin (erda)
max lorenz (siegfried)
erich zimmermann (mime)
rudolf bockelmann (wanderer)
robert burg (alberich)
josef von manowarda (fafner)

according to research by mike ashman, closing scene (heil dir sonne) existed in deutsches rundfunkarchiv

14/**19 july 1936**

lohengrin
edited excerpts from act three taken from the reichsrundfunk transmission

vorspiel, brautchor (treulich geführt) and brautgemach (das süsse lied verhallt)
bayreuth festival orchestra and chorus
conductor wilhelm furtwängler
chorus-master friedrich jung

lp: ed smith EJS 399
lp: cetra FE 25
lp: acanta HB 22 8630/40.23502/40.23520
lp: french furtwängler society SWF 7801-7803
cd: acanta 44.1055
cd: grammofono AB 78515
cd: iron needle IN 1634-1635
cd: archipel ARPCD 0284
cd: istituto discografico italiano IDIS 330-331
cd: venezia (japan) V 1024
also issued on cassette tape by house of opera (usa)

maria müller (elsa)
franz völker (lohengrin)

heil könig heinrich!......habt dank ihr lieben von brabant!
bayreuth festival orchestra and chorus
conductor wilhelm furtwängler
chorus-master friedrich jung

lp: ed smith EJS 399
lp: cetra FE 25
lp: acanta HB 22 8630/40.23502/40.23520
lp: french furtwängler society SWF 7801-7803
cd: acanta 44.1055
cd: fonoteam CD 74807
cd: grammofono AB 78515
cd: iron needle IN 1634-1635
cd: archipel ARPCD 0284
cd: istituto discografico italiano IDIS 330-331
cd: venezia (japan) V 1024
also issued on cassette tape by house of opera (usa)

josef von manowarda (könig heinrich)

19 july 1936/continued
in fernem land (gralserzählung)
bayreuth festival orchestra
conductor wilhelm furtwängler

lp: ed smith EJS 399
lp: cetra FE 25
lp: acanta 40.23502/40.23520
lp: french furtwängler society SWF 7801-7803
cd: acanta 44.1055
cd: fonoteam CD 74807
cd: grammofono AB 78515
cd: iron needle IN 1634-1635
cd: archipel ARPCD 0284
cd: istituto discografico italiano IDIS 330-331
cd: venezia (japan) V 1024
also issued on cassette tape by house of opera (usa)

franz völker (lohengrin)

mein lieber schwan

bayreuth festival orchestra and chorus
conductor wilhelm furtwängler
chorus-master friedrich jung

lp: ed smith EJS 399
lp: cetra FE 25
lp: acanta 40.23502
lp: french furtwängler society SWF 7801-7803
cd: acanta 44.1055
cd: fonoteam CD 74807
cd: grammofono AB 78515
cd: iron needle IN 1364-1365
cd: archipel ARPCD 0234
cd: istituto discografico italiano IDIS 330-331
cd: venezia (japan) V 1024
also issued on cassette tape by house of opera (usa)

franz völker (lohengrin)

19 july 1936/concluded
fahr heim du stolzer helde!....to end of act three
bayreuth festival orchestra and chorus
conductor wilhelm furtwängler
chorus-master friedrich jung

lp: ed smith EJS 399
lp: cetra FE 25
lp: acanta 40.23520
lp: french furtwängler society SWF 7801-7803
cd: acanta 44.1055
cd: fonoteam CD 78407
cd: grammofono AB 78515
cd: iron needle IN 1634-1635
cd: archipel ARPCD 0284
cd: istituto discografico italiano IDIS 330-331
cd: venezia (japan) V 1024
also issued on cassette tape by house of opera (usa)

maria müller (elsa)
margarete klose (ortrud)
franz völker (lohengrin)

15/20 august 1936
recordings made without audience by telefunken

siegfried: nothung neidliches schwert! (schmelzlied)
bayreuth festival orchestra
conductor heinz tietjen

78: telefunken SKB 02054
lp: telefunken KT 11017
cd: teldec 8573 830222/9031 764422
cd: malibran CDRG 109

max lorenz (siegfried)

siegfried: dass der mein vater nicht ist (waldweben)
bayreuth festival orchestra
conductor heinz tietjen

78: telefunken SKB 02055
lp: telefunken KT 11017
cd: teldec 8573 830222/9031 764422
cd: malibran CDRG 109
cd: myto MCD 93488
cd: archipel ARPCD 0186
myto and archipel editions incorrectly dated 1938

max lorenz (siegfried)

20 august 1936/continued
lohengrin: in fernem land (gralserzählung)
bayreuth festival orchestra
conductor heinz tietjen

78: telefunken SKB 02049
78: grammofon NSKB 02049
78: supraphon/ultraphon H 22622
lp: telefunken UV 241/HT 1/KT 11017/642.019
lp: scala (usa) 863
lp: top classic TC 9043
lp: deutsche grammophon 2721 062
cd: musica memoria 30283-30284
cd: memoir CDMOIR 405
cd: teldec 8573 830222/9031 764422
cd: malibran CDRG 109
cd: archipel ARPCD 0284

franz völker (lohengrin)

lohengrin: nun höret noch wie ich zu euch gekommen
this was the original reprise to in fernem land which wagner subsequently deleted from his score
bayreuth festival orchestra
conductor heinz tietjen

78: telefunken SKB 02049
78: grammofon NSKB 02049
lp: telefunken UV 241/HT 1/KT 11017/642.019
lp: scala (usa) 863
lp: top classic TC 9043
lp: deutsche grammophon 2721 062
cd: musica memoria 30283-30284
cd: memoir CDMOIR 405
cd: teldec 9031 764422
cd: malibran CDRG 109
cd: archipel ARPCD 0284

franz völker (lohengrin)

20 august 1936/continued
lohengrin: act three vorspiel and brautchor (treulich geführt)
bayreuth festival orchestra and chorus
conductor heinz tietjen
chorus-master friedrich jung

78: telefunken SKB 02051
lp: telefunken HT 11/KT 11017
cd: malibran CDREG 109
cd: archipel ARPCD 0284

lohengrin: brautgemach (das süsse lied verhallt...atmest du nicht mit mir die süssen düfte)
bayreuth festival orchestra
conductor heinz tietjen

78: telefunken SKB 02052
78: grammophon NSKB 02052
78: ultraphon H 22627
lp: telefunken HT 11/KT 11017/642.019
lp: preiser LV 81
cd: teldec 3984 269192/8573 830222/9031 764422
cd: musica memoria 30283-30284
cd: malibran CDREG 109
cd: archipel ARPCD 0284

maria müller (elsa)
franz völker (lohengrin)

16/**24 august 1936**
recordings made without sudience by telefunken

lohengrin: mein herr und gott! (königsgebet)
bayreuth festival orchestra and chorus
conductor heinz tietjen
chorus-master friedrich jung

78: telefunken SKB 02050
lp: telefunken HT 11/KT 11017
lp: emi 1C181 30669-30678M
cd: teldec 8573 830222/9031 764422
cd: victoria 290.242
cd: archipel ARPCD 0284

maria müller (elsa)
margarete klose (ortrud)
franz völker (lohengrin)
josef von manowarda (könig heinrich)
jaro prohaska (telramund)

lohengrin: gesegnet sollst du schreiten
bayreuth festival orchestra and chorus
conductor heinz tietjen
chorus-master friedrich jung

78: telefunken SKB 02050
cd: archipel ARPCD 0284

24 august 1936/concluded
**die walküre: winterstürme wichen dem wonnemond.....du bist der lenz
....siegmund heiss' ich!**
bayreuth festival orchestra
conductor heinz tietjen

78: telefunken SKB 02047-02048
78: grammophon NSKB 02047-02048
78: supraphon/ultraphon H 22623
lp: telefunken HT 11/KT 11017
lp: top classic TC 9043
lp: dg 410 8541
cd: teldec 8573 830222/9031 764422
cd: musica memoria 30285-30286
cd: malibran CDRG 109
cd: preiser 89235

maria müller (sieglinde)
franz völker (siegmund)

17/**26 august 1936**
recording made without audience by telefunken

siegfried: schmiede mein hammer! (schmiedelied)
bayreuth festival orchestra
conductor heinz tietjen

78: telefunken SKB 02054
lp: telefunken KT 11017
cd: teldec 8573 830222/9031 764422
cd: malibran CDRG 109

max lorenz (siegfried)
erich zimmermann (mime)

36
18/**29 august 1936**
recordings made without audience by telefunken

lohengrin: höchstes vertrau'n hast du schon mir zu danken
bayreuth festival orchestra
conductor heinz tietjen

78: telefunken SKB 02053
78: grammophon NSKB 02053
78: supraphon/ultraphon H 22628
lp: telefunken HT 1/KT 11017/642.019
cd: teldec 9031 764422
cd: malibran CDRG 109
cd: archipel ARPCD 0284

maria müller (elsa)
franz völker (lohengrin)

lohengrin: mein lieber schwan
bayreuth festival orchestra
conductor heinz tietjen

78: telefunken SKB 02053
78: grammophon NSKB 02053
78: supraphon/ultraphon H 22628
lp: telefunken HT 1/KT 11017/642.019
lp: scala (usa) 863
lp: fonit 75001
cd: teldec 9031 764422
cd: victoire 290.242
cd: musica memoria 30283-30284
cd: malibran CDRG 109
cd: archipel ARPCD 0284

franz völker (lohengrin)

19/august 1936
recordings made without audience by telefunken

die walküre: ein schwert verhiess mir der vater
bayreuth festival orchestra
conductor heinz tietjen

telefunken unpublished
matrix damaged

franz völker (siegmund)

der fliegende holländer: overture
bayreuth festival orchestra
conductor heinz tietjen

78: telefunken SKB 02089-02090
cd: malibran CDRG 109

20/27 july 1937
reichsrundfunk broadcast

die walküre: ein schwert verhiess mir der vater
bayreuth festival orchestra
conductor wilhelm furtwängler

unpublished reichsrundfunk recording
authenticity of this recording is doubted

max lorenz (siegmund)

21/30 july 1937
reichsrundfunk broadcast

götterdämmerung
bayreuth festival orchestra
and chorus
conductor wilhelm furtwängler
chorus-master friedrich jung

frida leider (brünnhilde)
maria müller (gutrune)
norma gadsden (waltraute)
max lorenz (siegfried)
jaro prohaska (gunther)
ludwig hofmann (hagen)
robert burg (alberich)
hilde scheppan (woglinde)
elfriede marherr (wellgunde & 3.norn))
rut berglund (flosshilde & 2.norn)
margarete klose (1.norn)

an lp of representative excerpts from this performance was published in 1978 by both discocorp and the french furtwängler society; however, this transpired to be a compilation of other recordings using mainly the same singers and the conductors wilhelm furtwängler and leo blech; discocorp simultaneously published an lp of extracts from parsifal including a supposed 1937 performance conducted by furtwängler

22/**july 1938**
reichsrundfunk broadcast

parsifal: nun achte wohl und lass mich seh'n
bayreuth festival orchestra and chorus
conductor franz von hoesslin
chorus-master friedrich jung

lp: acanta HB 22.8630/40.23502
authenticity of this recording is doubted by jonathan brown

josef von manowarda (gurnemanz)

23/**july 1939**
reichsrundfunk broadcast

tristan und isolde
bayreuth festival orchestra and chorus
conductor victor de sabata
chorus-master friedrich jung

early research had suggested that this recording had survived but this now seems unlikely: specially disappointing as de sabata was only the second italian conductor to have appeared at the festival after toscanini (excerpts published on lp by acanta and attributed to this performance were actually taken from a 1942 berlin performance conducted by robert heger)

germaine lubin (isolde)
margarete klose (brangäne)
max lorenz (tristan)
jaro prohaska (kurwenal)
josef von manowarda (marke)
fritz wolff (melot)
gustav rödin (hirt)
edwin heyer (steuermann)
benno arnold (junger seemann)

24/**17 june 1941**
reichsrundfunk broadcast

die walküre
bayreuth festival orchestra
conductor heinz tietjen

unpublished radio broadcast
excerpts from act one
lp: acanta HB 22.8630/40.23502
cd: hamburger archiv für gesangskunst HAGWAGNER 5
*complete performance announced by preiser but not so far published
(information from mike ashman)*

marta fuchs (brünnhilde)
maria müller (sieglinde)
margarete klose (fricka)
franz völker (siegmund)
rudolf bockelmann (wotan)
josef von manowarda (hagen)
irmgard langhammer (gerhilde)
elfriede marherr (ortlinde and siegrune)
ilse pfühl-jacobs (waltraute)
ilse bannog (schwertleite)
hilde scheppan (helmwige)
ria focke (grimgerde)
hill oswald-thoss (rossweisse)

25/**18 july 1942**
reichsrundfunk broadcast

der fliegende holländer
bayreuth festival orchestra and chorus
conductor richard kraus
chorus-master gerhard steeger

cd: preiser 90232
excerpts
lp: acanta 40.23502
cd: preiser 90364
cd: hamburger archiv für gesangskunst HAGWAGNER 2

maria müller (senta)
lilo asmus (mary)
joel berglund (holländer)
ludwig hofmann (daland)
franz völker (erik)
erich zimmermann (steuermann)

40
26/**21 july 1942**
reichsrundfunk broadcast

götterdämmerung
bayreuth festival orchestra and chorus
conductor karl elmendorff
chorus-master gerhard steeger

cd: preiser 90164
cd: music and arts CD 1058

marta fuchs (brünnhilde)
else fischer (gutrune)
camilla kallab (waltraute and 1.norn)
set svanholm (siegfried)
egmont koch (gunther)
friedrich dalberg (hagen)
robert burg (alberich)
hildegard jachnow (2.norn)
charlotte siewert (3.norn)
hilde scheppan (woglinde)
irmgard langhammer (wellgunde)
margery booth (flosshilde)

27/**15 july 1943**
reichsrundfunk broadcast

die meistersinger von nürnberg
bayreuth festival orchestra and chorus
conductor wilhelm furtwängler
chorus-master gerhard steeger

lp: ed smith UORC 266
lp: estro armonico EA 008
lp: foyer FO 1043
lp: emi 1C181 01797-01801M
cd: laudis LCD 44008
cd: dante LYS 026-029
cd: grammofono AB 78602-78605
cd: walhall WLCD 0050
cd: music and arts CD 1153
excerpts
lp: emi 1C181 30669-30678M
lp: acanta DE 23112-23113/40.23502
cd: acanta 44.1055
cd: history 20.3090/20.3092
cd: music and arts CD 794
opening scene of act one and quintet from act three are missing from the surviving tapes

maria müller (eva)
camilla kallab (magdalene)
max lorenz (stolzing)
erich zimmermann (david)
jaro prohaska (sachs)
josef greindl (pogner)
fritz krenn (kothner)
eugen fuchs (beckmesser)
benno arnold (vogelgesang)
helmut fehn (nachtigall)
gerhard witting (zorn)
gustav rödin (eisslinger)
karl krollmann (moser)
herbert gosebruch (ortel)
franz sauer (schwarz)
alfred dome (foltz)
erich pina (nachtwächter)

42
28/**16 july 1943**
reichsrundfunk broadcast

die meistersinger von nürnberg
bayreuth festival orchestra and chorus
conductor hermann abendroth
chorus-master gerhard steeger

cd: preiser 90174

hilde scheppan (eva)
camilla kallab (magdalene)
ludwig suthaus (stolzing)
erich witte (david)
paul schöffler (sachs)
friedrich dalberg (pogner)
erich kunz (beckmesser)
fritz krenn (kothner)
benno arnold (vogelgesang)
helmut fehn (nachtigall)
gerhard witting (zorn)
gustav rödin (eisslinger)
karl krollmann (moser)
herbert gosebtuch (ortel)
franz sauer (schwarz)
alfred dome (foltz)
erich pina (nachtwächter)

29/**july and august 1951**
recording made by columbia at dress rehearsal on 27 july and during performances between 5 august and 21 august

die meistersinger von nürnberg
bayreuth festival orchestra and chorus
conductor herbert von karajan
chorus-master wilhelm pitz

78: columbia LX 1465-1498/LX 8851-8884 auto
lp: columbia 33CX 1021-1025
lp: columbia (france) FCX 128-133
lp: columbia (austria) VCX 523-527
lp: columbia (germany) C 90275-90279/WCX 501-505
lp: angel seraphim 6030
lp: emi RLS 7708/RLS 143 3903/1C151 43390-43394M
cd: emi CHS 763 5002
cd: naxos 811.0872-0875
excerpts
78: columbia (austria) LVX 190-191
lp: emi 1C147 03580-03581M

elisabeth schwarzkopf (eva)
ira malaniuk (magdalene)
hans hopf (stolzing)
gerhard unger (david)
otto edelmann (sachs)
friedrich dalberg (pogner)
heinrich pflanzl (kothner)
erich kunz (beckmesser)
erich majkut (vogelgesang)
hans berg (nachtigall)
josef janko (zorn)
karl mikorey (eisslinger)
gerhard stolze (moser)
heinz tandler (ortel)
heinz borst (schwarz)
arnold van mill (foltz)
werner faulhaber (nachtwächter)

30/29 july 1951
performance marking both the re-opening and the seventy-fifth anniversary of the first bayreuth festival; broadcast by bayerischer rundfunk and subsequently published in 1955 by his master's voice

beethoven: symphony no 9 "choral"
bayreuth festival orchestra and chorus
conductor wilhelm furtwängler
chorus-master wilhelm pitz

lp: hmv ALP 1286-1287
lp: hmv (france) FALP 381-382/FALP 30048-30049/COLH 78-79/ UVT 3048-3049
lp: hmv (italy) QALP 10116-10117
lp: electrola E 90115-90116/WALP 1286-1287/EBE 600 000/ STE 90115-90116/SME 90115-90116/SMVP 3048-3049
lp: victor LM 6043
lp: angel 4003
lp: angel seraphim 6068
lp: emi RLS 727/1C147 00811-00812/1C149 53432-53439M/ 2C151 53678-53679/2C153 00811-00812/2C153 52540-52551/ 3C153 00811-00812
cd: emi CDC 747 0812/CDH 769 0812/CHS 763 6062/ CDM 566 9012/CHS 567 4962
also published on unofficial cd versions including membran and grand slam
final movement
lp: electrola E 80005/WALP 1508/WCLP 1508/SME 80005

elisabeth schwarzkopf
elisabeth höngen
hans hopf
otto edelmann

31/**30 july 1951**
decca recording compiled from this performance and subsequent ones in august; this performance also broadcast by bayerischer rundfunk

parsifal
bayreuth festival orchestra and chorus
conductor hans knappertsbusch
chorus-master wilhelm pitz

lp: decca LXT 2651-2656/GOM 504-508/411 7861
lp: london (usa) LLPA 10/A 4602/RS 65001
cd: teldec 9031 760472
cd: naxos 811.0221-0224
cd: membran 222.185444
excerpts
78: decca (switzerland) SX 63018-63030
lp: telefunken ND 523/BLK 16505
lp: discocorp IGI 379
issue of complete opera on cd by decca 425 9762 was announced but not released; IGI 379 was incorrectly described as from bayreuth in 1933

martha mödl (kundry)
wolfgang windgassen (parsifal)
george london (amfortas)
ludwig weber (gurnemanz)
hermann uhde (klingsor)
arnold van mill (titurel)
lore wissmann (1.blumenmädchen)
erika zimmermann (2.blumenmädchen)
hanna ludwig (3.blumenmädchen and 1.knappe)
paula brivkalne (4.blumenmädchen)
maria lacorn (5.blumenmädchen)
rut siewert (stimme von oben)
walter fritz (1.gralsritter)
werner faulhaber (2.gralsritter)
elfriede wild (2.knappe)
günther baldauf (3.knappe)
gerhard stolze (4.knappe)

32/**31 july 1951**
decca recording; performance also broadcast by bayerischer rundfunk

das rheingold
bayreuth festival orchestra
conductor hans knappertsbusch

decca unpublished

sigurd björling (wotan)
hanna ludwig (fricka and wellgunde)
paula brivkalne (freia)
rut siewert (erda)
werner faulhaber (donner)
wolfgang windgassen (froh)
walter fritz (loge)
heinrich pflamzl (alberich)
paul kuen (mime)
ludwig weber (fasolt)
friedrich dalberg (fafner)
elisabeth schwarzkopf (woglinde)
hertha töpper (flosshilde)

33/**1 august 1951**
decca recording

die walküre
bayreuth festival orchestra
conductor hans knappertsbusch

decca unpublished

astrid varnay (brünnhilde)
leonie rysanek (sieglinde)
hanna ludwig (fricka and rossweisse))
günther treptow (siegmund)
sigurd björling (wotan)
arnold van mill (hunding)
brünnhild friedland (gerhilde)
eleonor lausch (ortlinde)
elfriede wild (waltraute)
rut siewert (schwertleite)
lieselotte thomamüller (helmwige)
hertha töpper (siegrune)
ira malaniuk (grimgerde)

34/**2 august 1951**
decca recording

siegfried
bayreuth festival orchestra
conductor hans knappertsbusch

decca unpublished

bernd aldenhoff (siegfried)
sigurd björling (wanderer)
astrid varnay (brünnhilde)
wilma lipp (waldvogel)
rut siewert (erda)
paul kuen (mime)
heinrich pflanzl (alberich)
friedrich dalberg (fafner)

35/**4 august 1951**
decca recording

götterdämmerung
bayreuth festival orchestra and chorus
conductor hans knappertsbusch
chorus-master wilhelm pitz

cd: testament SBT 4175
cd: golden melodram GM 10067
excerpts
lp: private issue M 1043
cd: wing (japan) WCD 53

astrid varnay (brünnhilde)
martha mödl (gutrune and 3.norn)
elisabeth höngen (waltraute)
bernd aldenhoff (siegfried)
hermann uhde (gunther)
ludwig weber (hagen)
heinrich pflanzl (alberich)
elisabeth schwarzkopf (woglinde)
hanna ludwig (wellgunde)
hertha töpper (flosshilde)
rut siewert (1.norn)
ira malaniuk (2.norn)

36/**5 august 1951**
bayerischer rundfunk broadcast

die meistersinger von nürnberg
bayreuth festival orchestra and chorus
conductor herbert von karajan
chorus-master wilhelm pitz

cd: arkadia CDKAR 224
cd: documents 221743
cd: myto 022.H068
also published on cd by cantus classics

cast as for entry no. 29

37/**11 august 1951**
columbia recording and bayerischer rundfunk broadcast

das rheingold
bayreuth festival orchestra
conductor herbert von karajan

lp: melodram MEL 516
cd: walhall WLCD 0034
also published on lp by foyer and on cd by melodram and arkadia

sigurd björling (wotan)
ira malaniuk (fricka)
paula brivkalne (freia)
rut siewert (erda)
walter fritz (loge)
wolfgang windgassen (froh)
paul kuen (mime)
werner faulhaber (donner)
heinrich pflanzl (alberich)
ludwig weber (fasolt)
friedrich dalberg (fafner)
elisabeth schwarzkopf (woglinde)
lore wissmann (wellgunde)
hertha töpper (flosshilde)

38/**12 august 1951**
columbia recording

die walküre
bayreuth festival orchestra
conductor herbert von karajan

acts one and two
columbia unpublished
act three
78: columbia LX 1447-1454/LX 8835-8842 auto
lp: columbia 33CX 1005-1006
lp: columbia (germany) C 90280-90281
lp: emi 1C181 03035-03036M
cd: emi CDH 764 7042
excerpts
lp: emi 1C047 01373M

astrid varnay (brünnhilde)
leonie rysanek (sieglinde)
ira malaniuk (fricka and grimgerde)
günther treptow (siegmund)
sigurd björling (wotan)
arnold van mill (hunding)
brünnhild friedland (gerhilde)
eleonor lausch (ortlinde)
elfriede wild (waltraute)
rut siewert (schwertleite)
lieslotte thomamüller (helmwige)
hertha töpper (siegrune)
hanna ludwig (rossweisse)

39/**13 august 1951**
columbia recording

siegfried
bayreuth festival orchestra
conductor herbert von karajan

lp: melodram MEL 518
lp: foyer FO 1004
cd: arkadia CDKAR 219
cd: melodram MEL 46106
cd: walhall WLCD 0096
excerpts
cd: preiser 93437

astrid varnay (brünnhilde)
wilma lipp (waldvogel)
rut siewert (erda)
bernd aldenhoff (siegfried)
paul kuen (mime)
heinrich pflanzl (alberich)
friedrich dalberg (fafner)

40/**15 august 1951**
columbia recording

götterdämmerung
bayreuth festival orchesrra and chorus
conductor herbert von karajan
chorus-master wilhelm pitz

columbia unpublished

astrid varnay (brünnhilde)
martha mödl (gutrune and 3.norn)
rut siewert (waltraute and 1.norn)
bernd aldenhoff (siegfried)
hermann uhde (gunther)
ludwig weber (hagen)
heinrich pflanzl (alberich)
elisabeth schwarzkopf (woglinde)
lore wissmann (wellgunde)
hertha töpper (flosshilde)
ira malaniuk (2.norn)

41/23 july 1952
bayerischer rundfunk recording

tristan und isolde
bayreuth festival orchestra and chorus
conductor herbert von karajan
chorus-master wilhelm pitz

lp: discocorp IGI 291
lp: cetra LO 47
lp: foyer FO 1038
lp: melodram MEL 525
cd: arkadia CD 528
cd: myto MCD 962.149
cd: opera d'oro OPK 1173
cd: walhall WLCD 0096
cd: membran 221800
cd: urania DS 037502
cd: orfeo C603 033D
also published on cd by cantus classics
excerpts
lp: wg records WG 30010
lp: foyer FO 1034
lp: accord ACC 150 002
lp: longanesi GML 8
lp: ape records APE 1210
lp: replica RP 12704
lp: joker SM 1350
cd: classical collection CDCLC 6009
cd: de agostini CCL94 D41-2

martha mödl (isolde)
ira malaniuk (brangäne)
ramon vinay (tristan)
hans hotter (kurwenal)
ludwig weber (marke)
hermann uhde (melot)
werner faulhaber (steuermann)
gerhard stolze (hirt)
gerhard unger (junger seemann)

42/**1 august 1952**
bayerischer rundfunk broadcast

parsifal
bayreuth festival orchestra and chorus
conductor hans knapperetsbusch
chorus-master wilhelm pitz

cd: golden melodram GM 10051
cd: archipel ARPCD 0112
excerpts
lp: allegro-elite (usa) 3095
lp: gramophone (usa) 2090
allegro-elite and gramophone editions used pseudonyms for the performers

martha mödl (kundry)
wolfgang windgassen (parsifal)
ludwig weber (gurnemanz)
george london (amfortas)
hermann uhde (klingsor)
kurt böhme (titurel)
rut siewert (stimme von oben)
rita streich (1.blumenmädchen)
erika zimmermann (2.blumenmädchen)
hanna ludwig (3.blumenmädchen and 2.knappe)
paula brivkalne (4.blumenmädchen)
maria lacorne (5.blumenmädchen)
herta töpper (6.blumenmädchen and 1.knappe)
karl terkal (1.gralsritter)
werner faulhaber (2.gralsritter)
gerhard unger (3.knappe)
gerhard stolze (4.knappe)

43/**11 august 1952**
bayerischer rundfunk broadcast

das rheingold
bayreuth festival orchestra
conductor joseph keilberth

lp: melodram MEL 526
cd: paragon PCD 84015-84016
cd: archipel ARPCD 0113

hermann uhde (wotan)
ira malaniuk (fricka)
inge borkh (freia)
melanie bugarinovic (erda)
erich witte (loge)
wolfgang windgassen (froh)
paul kuen (mime)
werner faulhaber (donner)
gustav neidlinger (alberich)
ludwig weber (fasolt)
josef greindl (fafner)
erika zimmermann (woglinde)
hanna ludwig (wellgunde)
herta töpper (flosshilde)

44/**12 august 1952**
bayerischer rundfunk broadcast

die walküre
bayreuth festival orchestra
conductor joseph keilberth

lp: melodram MEL 527
cd: paragon PCD 84017-84020
cd: archipel ARPCD 0113
act one
lp: melodram MEL 077

astrid varnay (brünnhilde)
inge borkh (sieglinde)
ira malaniuk (fricka)
günther treptow (siegmund)
hans hotter (wotan)
josef greindl (hunding)
irmgard meinig (gerhilde)
paula brivkalne (ortlinde)
hanna ludwig (waltraute)
rut siewert (schwertleite)
lieselotte thomamüller (helmwige)
herta töpper (siegrune)
melanie bugarinovic (grimerde)
trude rösler (rossweisse)

bayerischer rundfunk now dates these broadcasts as 24 and 25 july 1952 (information from mike ashman)

45/**14 august 1952**
bayerischer rundfunk broascast

siegfried
bayreuth festival orchestra
conductor joseph keilberth

lp: melodram MEL 528
cd: paragon PCD 84021-84024
cd: archipel ARPCD 0113

astrid varnay (brünnhilde)
rita streich (waldvogel)
melanie bugarinovic (erda)
bernd aldenhoff (siegfried)
paul kuen (mime)
hans hotter (wanderer)
gustav neidlinger (alberich)
kurt boehme (fafner)

46/**16 august 1952**
bayerischer rundfunk broadcast

götterdämmerung
bayreuth festival orchestra and chorus
conductor joseph keilberth
chorus-master wilhelm pitz

lp: melodram MEL 529
cd: paragon PCD 84025-84028
cd: archipel ARPCD 0113

astrid varnay (brünnhilde)
martha mödl (gutrune and 3.norn)
rut siewert (waltraute and 1.norn)
max lorenz (siegfried)
hermann uhde (gunther)
josef geindl (hagen)
gustav neidlinger (alberich)
erika zimmermann (woglinde)
hanna ludwig (wellgunde)
herta töpper (flosshilde)
melanie bugarinovic (2.norn)

bayerischer rundfunk now dates these broadcasts as 27 and 29 july 1952
(information from mike ashman)

47/**17 august 1952**
bayerischer rundfunk broadcast

die meistersinger von nürnberg
bayreuth festival orchestra and chorus
conductor hans knappertsbusch
chorus-master wilhelm pitz

lp: melodram MEL 522
cd: arkadia CDLSMH 34040
cd: music and arts CD 1014
cd: golden melodram GM 10003
cd: archipel ARPCD 0111

lisa della casa (eva)
ira malaniuk (magdalene)
hans hopf (stolzing)
gerhard unger (david)
otto edelmann (sachs)
kurt böhme (pogner)
werner faulhaber (kothner)
heinrich pflamzl (beckmesser)
karl terkal (vogelgesang)
walter stoll (nachtigall)
josef jank (zorn)
karl mikorey (eisslinger)
gerhard stolze (moser)
theo adam (ortel)
heinz borst (schwarz)
max kohl (foltz)
gustav neidlinger (nachtwächter)

singer of role of eva was originally announced as trude eipperle, who may have sung some of the other performances in this year; bayerischer rundfunk now dates this broadcast as 3 august 1952 (information from mike ashman)

48/**23 july 1953**
*decca recording compiled from this performance and subsequent ones in july and august;
this performance also broadcast by bayerischer rundfunk*

lohengrin
bayreuth festival orchestra and chorus
conductor joseph keilberth
chorus-master wilhelm pitz

lp: decca LXT 2880-2884/D12 D5
lp: london (usa) A 4502/RS 65003
cd: teldec 4509 936742
cd: naxos 811.0308-0310
excerpts
lp: telefunken LW 50512/BLK 16514

eleanor steber (elsa)
astrid varnay (ortrud)
wolfgang windgassen (lohengrin)
hermann uhde (telramund)
josef greindl (könig heinrich)
hans braun (heerrufer)
gerhard stolze (1.edler)
josef janko (2.edler)
alfons herwig (3.edler)
theo adam (4.edler)

49/**24 july 1953**
bayerischer rundfunk broadcast

parsifal
bayreuth festival orchestra and chorus
conductor clemens krauss
chorus-master wilhelm pitz
clemens krauss replaced hans knappertsbusch as conductor

lp: documents OR 305
lp: melodram MEL 533
lp: rodolphe RP 12378-12381
cd: rodolphe RPC 32516-32517
cd: laudis LCD 44006
cd: arlecchino ARLA 18-21
cd: archipel ARPCD 0171
excerpts
lp: melodram MEL 650

martha mödl (kundry)
ramon vinay (parsifal)
george london (amfortas)
ludwig weber (gurnemanz)
hermann uhde (klingsor)
josef greindl (titurel)
rita streich (1.blumenmädchen)
erika zimmermann (2.blumenmädchen)
hetty plümacher (3.blumenmädchen and 1.knappe)
anna tassopoulos (4.blumenmädchen)
gerda wismat (5.blumenmädchen)
gisela litz (6.blumenmädchen and 2.knappe)
maria von ilosvay (stimme von oben)
eugene tobin (1.gralsritter)
theo adam (2.gralsritter)
hugo kratz (3.knappe)
gerhard stolze (4.knappe)

50/25 july 1953
bayrerischer rundfunk broadcast

das rheingold
bayreuth festival orchestra
conductor joseph keilberth

lp: allegro-elite 3125-3127
lp: melodram MEL 536
cd: golden melodram GM 10014
cd: andromeda ANDRCD 5000
allegro-elite edition used pseudonyms

hans hotter (wotan)
ira malaniuk (fricka)
bruni falcon (freia)
maria von ilosvay (erda)
erich witte (loge)
gerhard stolze (froh)
paul kuen (mime)
hermann uhde (donner)
gustav neidlinger (alberich)
ludwig weber (fasolt)
josef greindl (fafner)
erika zimmermann (woglinde)
hetty plümacher (wellgunde)
gisela litz (flosshilde)

51/26 july 1953
bayerischer rundfunk broadcast

die walküre
bayreuth festival orchestra
conductor joseph keilberth

lp: allegro-elite 3128-3132
lp: melodram MEL 537
cd: golden melodram GM 10014
cd: andromeda ANDRCD 5000
allegro-elite edition used pseudonyms

martha mödl (brünnhilde)
regina resnik (sieglinde)
ira malaniuk (fricka)
ramon vinay (siegmund)
hans hotter (wotan)
josef greindl (hunding)
brünnhilde friedland (gerhilde)
bruni falcon (ortlinde)
ilse sorrell (waltraute)
maria von ilosvay (schwertleite)
lieselotte thomamüller (helmwige)
gisela litz (siegrune)
sybilla plate (grimgerde)
erika schubert (rossweisse)

52/**27 july 1953**
bayerischer rundfunk broadcast

siegfried
bayreuth festival orchestra
conductor joseph keilberth

lp: allegro-elite 3133-3137
lp: melodram MEL 538
cd: golden melodram GM 10014
cd: andromeda ANDRCD 5000
allegro-elite edition used pseudonyms

martha mödl (brünnhilde)
rita streich (waldvogel)
maria von ilosvay (erda)
wolfgang windgassen (siegfried)
paul kuen (mime)
hans hotter (wanderer)
gustav neidlinger (alberich)
josef greindl (fafner)

53/**29 july 1953**
bayerischer rundfunk broadcast

götterdämmerung
bayreuth festival orchestra and chorus
conductor joseph keilberth
chorus-master wilhelm pitz

lp: allegro-elite 3138-3142
lp: melodram MEL 539
cd: golden melodram GM 10014
cd: andromeda ANDRCD 5000
allegro-elite edition used pseudonyms

martha mödl (brünnhilde)
natalie hinsch-gröndahl (gutrune)
ira malaniuk (waltraute)
wolfgang windgassen (siegfried)
hermann uhde (gunther)
josef greindl (hagen)
gustav neidlinger (alberich)
erika zimmermann (woglinde)
hetty plümacher (wellgunde)
gisela litz (flosshilde)
maria von ilosvay (1.norn)
ira malaniuk (2.norn)
regina resnik (3.norn)

54/**30 july 1953**
bayerischer rundfunk broadcast

tristan und isolde
bayreuth festival orchestra and chorus
conductor eugen jochum
chorus-master wilhelm pitz

lp: documents OR 301
lp: melodram MEL 535
cd: arkadia CDLSMH 34030
cd: golden melodram GM 10030
cd: archipel ARPCD 0170

astrid varnay (isolde)
ira malaniuk (brangäne)
ramon vinay (tristan)
gustav neidlinger (kurwenal)
ludwig weber (marke)
hanno eschert (melot)
gerhard stolze (hirt)
theo adam (steuermann)
eugene tobin (ein junger seemann)

55/**8 august 1953**
bayerischer rundfunk broadcast

das rheingold
bayreuth festival orchestra
conductor clemens krauss
*clemens krauss replaced hans
knappertsbusch as conductor*

lp: foyer FO 1008
cd: foyer 3CF 2007/15CF 2011
cd: rodolphe RPC 32503-32509
cd: gala GL 999.791/GL 100.651
cd: archipel ARPCD 0250

cast as for entry no. 50

56/**9 august 1953**
bayerischer rundfunk broadcast

die walküre
bayreuth festival orchestra
conductor clemens krauss
*clemens krauss replaced hans
knappertsbusch as conductor*

lp: foyer FO 1009
cd: foyer 4CF 2008/15CF 2011
cd: rodolphe RPC 32503-32509
cd: gala GL 999.791/GL 100.652
cd: archipel ARPCD 0250

*astrid varnay (brünnhilde)
rest of cast as for entry no. 51*

57/**10 august 1953**
bayerischer rundfunk broadcast

siegfried
bayreuth festival orchestra
conductor clemens krauss
*clemens krauss replaced hans
knappertsbusch as conductor*

lp: foyer FO 1010
cd: foyer 4CF 2009/15CF 2011
cd: rodolphe RPC 32503-32509
cd: gala GL 999.791/GL 100.653
cd: archipel ARPCD 0250

*astrid varnay (brünnhilde)
rest of cast as for entry no. 52*

58/**11 august 1953**
bayerischer rundfunk broadcast

beethoven: symphony no 9   "choral"
bayreuth festival orchestra and chorus
conductor paul hindemith
chorus-master wilhelm pitz

unpublished radio brodcast
*according to mike ashman bayerischer rundfunk reports that this tape
is no longer held in their archive*

birgit nilsson
ira malaniuk
anton dermota
ludwig weber

59/**12 august 1953**
bayerischer rundfunk broadcast

götterdämmerung
bayreuth festival orchestra and chorus
conductor clemens krauss
chorus-master wilhelm pitz
clemens krauss replaced hans knappertsbusch as conductor

lp: foyer FO 1011
cd: foyer 4CF 2010/15CF 2011
cd: rodolphe RPC 32503-32509
cd: gala GL 999.791/GL 100.654
cd: archipel ARPCD 0250

astrid varnay (brünnhilde)
rest of cast as for entry no. 53

60/22 july 1954
bayerischer rundfunk broadcast

tannhäuser
bayreuth festival orchestra and chorus
conductor joseph keilberth
chorus-master wilhelm pitz
joseph keilberth replaced igor markevitch as conductor

lp: melodram MEL 544
cd: melodram MEL 36105
cd: golden melodram GM 10032
cd: archipel ARPCD 0280
excerpts
lp: gioielli della lirica GML 027

gré brouwenstijn (elisabeth)
herta wilfert (venus)
ramon vinay (tannhäuser)
josef geindl (landgraf)
dietrich fischer-dieskau (wolfram)
josef traxel (walther von der vogelweide)
gerhard stolze (heinrich der schreiber)
toni blankenheim (biterolf)
theo adam (reinmar von zweter)
volker horn (ein junger hirt)

64

61/**24 july 1954**
bayerischer rundfunk broadcast

das rheingold
bayreuth festival orchestra
conductor joseph keilberth

unpublished radio broadcast

hans hotter (wotan)
georgine von milinkovic (fricka)
herta wilfert (freia)
maria von ilosvay (erda)
rudolf lustig (loge)
josef traxel (froh)
paul kuen (mime)
toni blankenheim (donner)
gustav neidlinger (alberich)
ludwig weber (fasolt)
josef greindl (fafner)
erika zimmermann (woglinde)
hetty plümacher (wellgunde)
gisela litz (flosshilde)

62/**25 july 1954**
bayerischer rundfunk broadcasr

die walküre
bayreuth festival orchestra
conductor joseph keilberth

lp: melodram MEL 547
cd: melodram MEL 36102/GM 10065
cd: archipel ARPCD 0282

astrid varnay (brünnhilde)
martha mödl (sieglinde)
georgine von milinkovic (fricka and grimgerde)
max lorenz (siegmund)
hans hotter (wotan)
josef greindl (hunding)
herta wilfert (gerhilde)
birgit nilsson (ortlinde)
elisabeth schärtel (waltraute)
maria von ilosvay (schwertleite)
hilde scheppan (helmwige)
gisela litz (siegrune)
hetty plümacher (rossweisse)

63/**26 july 1954**
bayerischer rundfunk broadcast

siegfried
bayreuth festival orchestra
conductor joseph keilberth

unpublished radio broadcast

astrid varnay (brünnhilde)
ilse hollweg (waldvogel)
maria von ilosvay (erda)
wolfgang windgassen (siegfried)
paul kuen (mime)
hans hotter (wanderer)
gustav neidlinger (alberich)
josef greindl (fafner)

64/**28 july 1954**
bayerischer rundfunk broadcast

götterdämmerung
bayreuth festival orchestra
and chorus
conductor joseph keilberth
chorus-master wilhelm pitz

unpublished radio broadcast

astrid varnay (brünnhilde)
martha mödl (gutrune)
maria von ilosvay (waltraute and 1.norn)
wolfgang windgassen (siegfried)
hermann uhde (gunther)
josef greindl (hagen)
gustav neidlinger (alberich)
erika zimmermann (woglinde)
hetty plümacher (wellgunde)
gisela litz (flosshilde)
georgine von milinkovic (2.norn)
mina bolotine (3.norn)

65/**4 august 1954**
bayerischer rundfunk broadcast

lohengrin
bayreuth festival orchestra and chorus
conductor eugen jochum
chorus-master wilhelm pitz

lp: cetra LO 77
lp: melodram MEL 541
cd: laudis LCD 44015
cd: melodram MEL 36104
cd: golden melodram GM 10031
cd: archipel ARPCD 0281
also issued on cassette tape by house of opera (usa)
excerpts
lp: gioielli della lirica GML 20
cd: memories HR 4424-4425

birgit nilsson (elsa)
astrid varnay (ortrud)
wolfgang windgassen (lohengrin)
hermann uhde (telramund)
theo adam (könig heinrich)
dietrich fischer-dieskau (heerrufer)
gerhard stolze (1.edler)
eugene tobin (2.edler)
toni blankenheim (3.edler)
franz crass (4.edler)

bayerischer rundfunk now dates this broadcast as 23 july 1954 (information from mike ashman); house of opera issue incorrectly dated 1 august 1954

66/8 august 1954
recording of rehearsal performance from a private archive

beethoven: symphony no 9 "choral"
third and fourth movements only
bayreuth festival orchestra and chorus
conductor wilhelm furtwängler
chorus-master wilhelm pitz

lp: private issue (japan) AT 07-08
cd: refrain (japan) DR 92 0033
cd: venezia (japan) V 1024
cd: wilhelm furtwängler centre japan WFHC 001-002

gré brouwenstijn
ira malaniuk
wolfgang windgassen
ludwig weber

67/9 august 1954
bayerischer rundfunk broadcast

beethoven: symphony no 9 "choral"
bayreuth festival orchestra and chorus
conductor wilhelm furtwängler
chorus-master wilhelm pitz

lp: private issue (japan) W 16
cd: refrain (japan) DR 91 0016
cd: wilhelm furtwängler centre japan WFHC 001-002
cd: music and arts CD 1127
music and arts edition incorrectly dated 8 august

gré brouwenstijn
ira malaniuk
wolfgang windgassen
ludwig weber

according to mike ashman bayerischer rundfunk reports that this tape is no longer held in their archive

68
68/**17 august 1954**
bayerischer rundfunk broadcast

parsifal
bayreuth festival orchestra and chorus
conductor hans knappertsbusch
chorus-master wilhelm pitz

cd: archipel ARPCD 0283
excerpts
lp: melodram MEL 583/MEL 643
melodram issues dated 1956 and 5 august 1954 respectively

martha mödl (kundry)
wolfgang windgassen (parsifal)
hans hotter (amfortas)
josef greindl (gurnemanz)
gustav neidlinger (klingsor)
theo adam (titurel and 2.gralsritter)
hetty plümacher (stimme von oben, 3.blumenmädchen and 1.knappe)
ilse hollweg (1.blumenmädchen)
friedl pöltinger (2.blumenmädchen)
dorothea siebert (4.blumenmädchen)
jutta vulpius (5.blumenmädchen)
gisela litz (6.blumenmädchen and 2.knappe)
eugene tobin (1.gralsritter)
gerhard stolze (3.knappe)
hugo kratz (4.knappe)

69/27 april 1955/barcelona teatro del liceu
recording of a guest performance by the bayreuth festival

die walküre
bamberg symphony orchestra
conductor joseph keilberth

cd: walhall WLCD 0154
also issued on cassette tape by house of opera (usa)

martha mödl (brünnhilde)
gré brouwenstijn (sieglinde)
georgine von milinkovic (fricka and grimgerde)
wolfgang windgassen (siegmund)
hans hotter (wotan)
josef greindl (hunding)
hertha wilfert (gerhilde)
mina bolotine (ortlinde)
elisabeth schärtel (waltraute)
trude roesler (schwertleite)
hilde scheppan (helmwige)
erika schubert (siegrune)
betty plümacher (rossweisse)

this gastspiel in barcelona also included performances of parsifal and tristan und isolde

70
70/**22 july 1955**
bayerischer rundfunk broadcast

der fliegende holländer
bayreuth festival orchestra and chorus
conductor hans knappertsbusch
chorus-master wilhelm pitz

lp: cetra LO 51
lp: discocorp IGI 319
lp: melodram MEL 550
cd: arkadia CDLSMH 34021
cd: music and arts CD 319/CD 876
cd: golden melodram GM 10028
cd: urania URN 22271
cd: walhall WLCD 0161
excerpts
lp: melodram MEL 094

astrid varnay (senta)
elisabeth schärtel (mary)
hermann uhde (holländer)
wolfgang windgassen (erik)
josef traxel (steuermann)
ludwig weber (daland)

according to mike ashman bayerischer rundfunk states that this tape is no longer stored in their archive

71/24 july 1955
decca recording

das rheingold
bayreuth festival orchestra
conductor joseph keilberth

cd: testament SBT2 1390
audiophile lp: testament
   SBTLP3 1390

hans hotter (wotan)
georgine von milinkovic (fricka)
herta wilfert (freia)
maria von ilosvay (erda)
rudolf lustig (loge)
josef traxel (froh)
paul kuen (mime)
toni blankenheim (donner)
gustav neidlinger (alberich)
ludwig weber (fasolt)
josef greindl (fafner)
jutta vulpius (woglinde)
elisabeth schärtel (wellgunde)
maria graf (flosshilde)

72/25 july 1955
decca recording

die walküre
bayreuth festival orchestra
conductor joseph keilberth

cd: testament SBT4 1391
audiophile lp: testament
   SBTLP5 1391

astrid varnay (brünnhilde)
gré brouwenstijn (sieglinde)
georgine von milinkovic (fricka & grimgerde)
ramon vinay (siegmund)
hans hotter (wotan)
josef greindl (hunding)
herta wilfert (gerhilde)
gerda lammers (ortlinde)
elisabeth schärtel (waltraute)
maria von ilosvay (schwertleite)
hilde scheppan (helmwige)
jean watson (siegrune)
maria graf (rossweisse)

73/26 july 1955
decca recording

siegfried
bayreuth festival orchestra
conductor joseph keilberth

cd: testament SBT4 1392
audiophile lp: testament
   SBTLP5 1392

astrid varnay (brünnhilde)
ilse hollweg (waldvogel)
maria von ilosvay (erda)
wolfgang windgassen (siegfried)
paul kuen (mime)
hans hotter (wanderer)
gustav neidlinger (alberich)
josef greindl (fafner)

74/28 july 1955
decca recording

götterdämmerung
bayreuth festival orchestra and chorus
conductor joseph keilberth
chorus-master wilhelm pitz

cd: testament SBT4 1393
audiophile lp: testament
   SBTLP5 1393

astrid varnay (brünnhilde)
gré brouwenstijn (gutrune)
maria von ilosvay (waltraute and 1.norn)
wolfgang windgassen (siegfried)
hermann uhde (gunther)
josef greindl (hagen)
gustav neidlinger (alberich)
jutta vulpius (woglinde)
elisabeth schärtel (wellgunde)
maria graf (flosshilde)
georgine von milinkovic (2.norn)
mina bolotine (3.norn)

75/7 august 1955
decca recording and bayerischer rundfunk broadcast

der fliegende holländer
bayreuth festival orchestra and chorus
conductor joseph keilberth
chorus-master wilhelm pitz

lp: decca LXT 5150-5152/D97 D3/ECS 665-667
lp: london (usa) A 4325
cd: teldec 4509 974912
cd: testament awaiting publication
excerpts
lp: telefunken BLK 16513

astrid varnay (senta)
elisabeth schärtel (mary)
hermann uhde (holländer)
rudolf lustig (erik)
josef traxel (steuermann)
ludwig weber (daland)

76/9 august 1955
bayerischer rundfunk broadcast

tannhäuser
bayreuth festival orchestra and chorus
conductor andré cluytens
chorus-master wilhelm pitz
andré cluytens replaced eugen jochum as conductor

cd: orfeo C643 043D
cd: walhall WLCD 0162
also issued on cd by golden melodram

gré brouwenstijn (elisabeth)
herta wilfert (venus)
wolfgang windgassen (tannhäuser)
josef greindl (landgraf)
dietrich fischer-dieskau (wolfram)
josef traxel (walther von der vogelweide)
gerhard stolze (heinrich der schreiber)
toni blankenheim (biterolf)
alfons herwig (reinmar von zweter)
volker horn (ein junger hirt)

77/**10 august 1955**
*decca recording and nayerischer
rundfunk broadcast*

das rheingold
bayreuth festival orchestra
conductor joseph keilberth

decca unpublished

cast as for entry no. 71

78/**11 august 1955**
*decca recording and bayerischer
rundfunk broadcast*

die walküre
bayreuth festival orchestra
conductor joseph keilberth

lp: melodram MEL 557
*melodram issue was incorrectly dated
dated 25 july 1955*

*maerha mödl (brünnhilde)
astrid varnay (sieglinde)
rest of cast as for enrey no. 72*

79/**12 august 1955**
*decca recording and bayerischer
rundfunk broadcast*

siegfried
bayreuth festival orchestra
conductor joseph keilberth

decca unpublished

*martha mödl (brünnhilde)
rest of cast as for entry no. 73*

80/**14 august 1955**
*decca recording and bayerischer
rundfunk broadcast*

götterdämmerung
bayreuth festival orchestra and chorus
conductor joseph keilberth
chorus-master wilhelm pitz

cd: testament awaiting publication

*martha mödl (brünnhilde)
astrid varnay (3.norn)
hans hotter (gunther)
rest of cast as for entry no. 74*

81/16 august 1955
bayerischer rundfunk broadcast

parsifal
bayreuth festival orchestra and chorus
conductor hans knappertsbusch
chorus-master wilhelm pitz

unpublished radio broadcast

martha mödl (kundry and stimme von oben)
ramon vinay (parsifal)
dietrich fischer-dieskau (amfortas)
ludwig weber (gurnemanz)
gustav neidlinger (klingsor)
hermann uhde (titurel)
ilse hollweg (1.blumenmädchen)
friedl pöltinger (2.blumenmädchen)
paula lenchner (3.blumenmädchen and 1.knappe)
dorothea siebert (4.blumenmädchen)
jutta vulpius (5.blumenmädchen)
elisabeth schärtel (6.blumenmädchen and 2.knappe)
josef traxel (1.gralsritter)
alfons herwig (2.gralsritter)
alfred pfeifle (3.knappe)
gerhard stolze (4.knappe)

82/**24 july 1956**
bayerischer rundfunk broadcast

die meistersinger von nürnberg
bayreuth festival orchestra and chorus
conductor andré cluytens
chorus-master wilhelm pitz

cd: music and arts CD 1011

gré brouwenstijn (eva)
georgine von milinkovic (magdalene)
wolfgang windgassen (stolzing)
gerhard stolze (david)
hans hotter (sachs)
josef greindl (pogner)
dietrich fischer-dieskau (kothner)
karl schmitt-walter (beckmesser)
josef traxel (vogelgesang)
egmont koch (nachtigall)
heinz-günther zimmermann (zorn)
erich benke (eisslonger)
josef janko (moser)
hans habietinek (ortel)
alexander fenyves (schwarz)
eugen fuchs (foltz)
alfons herwig (nachtwächter)

according to mike ashman bayerischer rundfunk states that this tape is no longer held in their archive

83/**25 july 1956**
bayerischer rundfunk broadcast

der fliegende holländer
bayreuth festival orchestra and chorus
conductor joseph keilberth
chorus-master wilhelm pitz

lp: melodram MEL 560
cd: myto MCD 93175
excerpts
cd: opernwelt 2002

astrid varnay (senta)
elisabeth schärtel (mary)
george london (holländer)
josef traxel (erik)
jean cox (steuermann)
arnold van mill (daland)

according to mike ashman bayerischer rundfunk states that this tape is no longer held in their archive

84/**12 august 1956**
bayerischer rundfunk broadcast

der fliegende holländer
bayreuth festival orchestra
conductor joseph keilberth

unpublished radio broadcast
exceerpts
lp: melodram MEL 560

astrid varnay (senta)
elisabeth schärtel (mary)
paul schöffler (holländer)
josef traxel (erik)
jean cox (steuermann)
ludwig weber (daland)

bayerischer rundfunk incorrectly states that the singer of holländer at this performance was george london

85/**13 august 1956**
bayerischer rundfunk broadcast

das rheingold
bayreuth festival orchestra
conductor hans knappertsbusch

cd: music and arts CD 1009/
   CD 4009
cd: golden melodram GM 1001
cd: orfeo C660 513Y
previous cd issue by king records in japan; golden melodram issue in collaboration with the hans-knappertsbusch-gesellschaft

hans hotter (wotan)
georgine von milinkovic (fricka)
gré brouwenstijn (freia)
jean madeira (erda)
ludwig suthaus (loge)
josef traxel (froh)
paul kuen (mime)
alfons herwig (donner)
gustav neidlinger (alberich)
josef greindl (fasolt)
arnold van mill (fafner)
lore wissmann (woglinde)
paula lenchner (wellgunde)
maria von ilosvay (flosshilde)

86/**14 august 1956**
bayerischer rundfunk broadcast

die walküre
bayreuth festival orchestra
conductor hans knappertsbusch

lp: melodram MEL 567
cd: music and arts CD 1009/
   CD 4009
cd: golden melodram GM 1001
cd: orfeo C660 513Y
previous cd issue by king records in japan: golden melodram issue in collaboration with the hans-knappertsbusch-gesellschaft

astrid varnay (brünnhilde)
gré brouwenstijn (sieglinde)
georgine von milinkovic (fricka & grimgerde)
wolfgang windgassen (siegmund)
hans hotter (wotan)
josef greindl (hunding)
paula lenchner (gerhilde)
gerda lammers (ortlinde)
elisabeth schärtel (waltraute)
maria von ilosvay (schwertleite)
hilde scheppan (helmwige)
luise charlotte kamps (siegrune)
jean madeira (rossweisse)

87/**15 august 1956**
bayerischer rundfunk broadcast

siegfried
bayreuth festival orchestra
conductor hans knappertsbusch

cd: music and arts CD 1009/
 CD 4009
cd: golden melodram GM 1001
cd: orfeo C660 513Y

previous cd issue by king records in japan; golden melodram issue in collaboration with the hans-knappertsbusch-gesellschaft

astrid varnay (brünnhilde)
ilse hollweg (waldvogel)
jean madeira (erda)
wolfgang windgassen (siegfried)
paul kuen (mime)
hans hotter (wanderer)
gustav neidlinger (alberich)
arnold van mill (fafner)

88/**17 august 1956**
bayerischer rundfunk broadcast

götterdämmerung
bayreuth festival orchestra and chorus
conductor hans knappertsbusch
chorus-master wilhelm pitz

lp: melodram MEL 569
cd: music and arts CD 1009/
 CD 4009
cd: golden melodram GM 1001
cd: orfeo C660 513Y
excerpts
cd: music and arts CD 319

previous cd issue by king records in japan; golden melodram issue in collaboration with the hans-knappertsbusch-gesellschaft

astrid varnay (brünnhilde and 3.norn)
gré brouwenstijn (gutrune)
jean madeira (waltraute and 1.norn)
wolfgang windgassen (siegfried)
hermann uhde (gunther)
josef greindl (hagen)
gustav neidlinger (alberich)
lore wissmann (woglinde)
paula lenchner (wellgunde)
maria von ilosvay (flosshilde and 2.norn)

89/**18 august 1956**
bayerischer rundfunk broadcast

die meistersinger von nürnberg
bayreuth festival orchestra
conductor andré cluytens
chorus-master wilhelm pitz

unpublished radio broadcast

lore wissmann (eva)
gustav neidlinger (sachs)
rest of cast as for entry no. 82

90/**19 august 1956**
bayerischer rundfunk broadcast

parsifal
bayreuth festival orchestra and chorus
conductor hans knappertsbusch
chorus-master wilhelm pitz

lp: cetra LO 79
lp: melodram MEL 563
cd: arkadia CDLSMH 34035
cd: golden melodram GM 10062
excerpts
lp: gioielli della lirica GML 43
GML 43 incorrectly dated july 1956

martha mödl (kundry and stimme von oben)
ramon vinay (parsifal)
dietrich fischer-dieskau (amfortas)
josef greindl (gurnemanz)
hans hotter (titurel)
toni blankenheim (klingsor)
ilse hollweg (1.blumenmädchen)
friedl pöltinger (2.blumenmädchen)
paula lenchner (3.blumenmädchen and 1.knappe)
dorothea siebert (4.blumenmädchen)
jutta vulpius (5.blumenmädchen)
elisabeth schärtel (6.blumenmädchen and 2.knappe)
josef traxel (1.gralsritter)
alfons herwig (2.gralsritter)
gerhard stolze (3.knappe)
alfred pfeifle (4.knappe)

91/**23 july 1957**
bayerischer rundfunk broascast

tristan und isolde
bayreuth festival orchestra
and chorus
conductor wolfgang sawallisch
chorus-master wilhelm pitz

unpublished radio broadcast

birgit nilsson (isolde)
grace hoffman (brangäne)
wolfgang windgassen (tristan)
gustav neidlinger (kurwenal)
arnold van mill (marke)
fritz uhl (melot)
hermann winkler (hirt)
egmont koch (steuermann)
josef traxel (ein junger seemann)

92/**24 july 1957**
bayerischer rundfunk broadcast

die meistersinger von nürnberg
bayreuth festival orchestra
and chorus
conductor andré cluytens
chorus-master wilhelm pitz

unpublished radio broadcast

elisabeth grümmer (eva)
josef traxel (stolzing)
otto wiener (sachs)
gottlob frick (pogner)
toni blankenheim (kothner)
hermann winkler (moser)
arnold van mill (nachtwächter)
rest of cast as foe entry no. 82

93/**13 august 1957**
bayerischer rundfunk broadcast

parsifal
bayreuth festival orchestra and chorus
conductor andré cluytens
chorus-master wilhelm pitz

unpublished radio broadcast

martha mödl (kundry)
ramon vinay (parsifal)
josef greindl (gurnemanz)
george london (amfortas)
arnold van mill (titurel)
toni blankenheim (klingsor)
georgine von milinkovic (stimme von oben)
ilse hollweg (1.blumenmädchen)
friedl pöltinger (2.blumenmädchen)
paula lenchner (3.blumenmädchen and 1.knappe)
dorothea siebert (4.blumenmädchen)
lotte rysanek (5.blumenmädchen)
elisabeth schärtel (6.blumenmädchen and 2.knappe)
walter geisler (1.gralsritter)
otto wiener (2.gralsritter)
hans krotthammer (3.knappe)
gerhard stolze (4.knappe)

94/**14 august 1957**
bayerischer rundfunk broadcast

das rheingold
bayreuth festival orchestra
conductor hans knappertsbusch

lp: estro armonico EA 031
lp: discocorp IGI 292
lp: cetra LO 58/DOC 47
lp: melodram MEL 576
cd: music and arts CD 253
cd: laudis LCD 44010/154 021
cd: golden melodram GM 10048

hans hotter (wotan)
georgine von milinkovic (fricka)
elisabeth grümmer (freia)
maria von ilosvay (erda)
ludwig suthaus (loge)
josef traxel (froh)
gerhard stolze (mime)
toni blankenheim (donner)
gustav neidlinger (alberich)
arnold van mill (fasolt)
josef greindl (fafner)
dorothea siebert (woglinde)
paula lenchner (wellgunde)
elisabeth schärtel (flosshilde)

95/**15 august 1957**
bayerischer rundfunk broadcast

die walküre
bayreuth festival orchestra
conductor hans knappertsbusch

lp: estro armonico EA 032
lp: discocorp IGI 292
lp: cetra LO 59/DOC 48
lp: melodram MEL 577
cd: music and arts CD 254
cd: laudis LCD 44011/154 021
cd: golden melodram GM 10048

astrid varnay (brünnhilde)
birgit nilsson (sieglinde)
georgine von milinkovic (fricka & grimgerde)
ramon vinay (siegmund)
hans hotter (wotan)
josef greindl (hunding)
paula lenchner (gerhilde)
gerda lammers (ortlinde)
elisabeth schärtel (waltraute)
maria von ilosvay (schwertleite)
hilde scheppan (helmwige)
helena bader (siegrune)
hetty plümacher (rossweisse)

96/**16 august 1957**
bayerischer rundfunk broadcast

siegfried
bayreuth festival orchestra
conductor hans knappertsbusch

lp: estro armonico EA 033
lp: discocorp IGI 292
lp: cetra LO 60/DOC 49
lp: melodram MEL 578
cd: music and arts CD 255
cd: laudis LCD 44012/154 021
cd: golden melodram GM 10048

astrid varnay (brünnhilde)
ilse hollweg (waldvogel)
maria von ilosvay (erda)
bernd aldenhoff (siegfried)
paul kuen (mime)
hans hotter (wanderer)
gustav neidlinger (alberich)
josef greindl (fafner)

97/**18 august 1957**
bayerischer rundfunk broadcast

götterdämmerung
bayreuth festival orchestra and chorus
conductor hans knappertsbusch
chorus-master wilhelm pitz

lp: estro armonico EA 034
lp: discocorp IGI 292
lp: cetra LO 61/DOC 50
lp: melodram MEL 579
cd: music and arts CD 256
cd: laudis LCD 44013/154 021
cd: golden melodram GM 10048

astrid varnay (brünnhilde)
elisabeth grümmer (gutrune)
maria von ilosvay (waltraute and 1.norn)
wolfgang windgassen (siegfried)
hermann uhde (gunther)
josef greindl (hagen)
gustav neidlinger (alberich)
dorothea siebert (woglinde)
paula lenchner (wellgunde)
elisabeth schärtel (flosshilde and 2.norn)
birgit nilsson (3.norn)

98/**19 august 1957**
bayerischer rundfunk broadcast

tristan und isolde
bayreuth festival orchestra and chorus
conductor wolfgang sawallisch
chorus-master wilhelm pitz

lp: melodram MEL 575
cd: golden melodram GM 10020

hans hotter (kurwenal)
walter geisler (ein junger seemann)
rest of cast as for entry no. 91

99/**20 august 1957**
bayerischer rundfunk broadcast

die meistersinger von nürnberg
bayreuth festival orchestra and chorus
conductor andré cluytens
chorus-master wilhelm pitz

lp: melodram MEL 572
melodram issue incorrectly dated 24 july 1957

elisabeth grümmer (eva)
walter geisler (stolzing)
gustav neidlinger (sachs)
toni blankenheim (kothner)
hermann winkler (moser)
arnold van mill (nachtwächter)
rest of cast as for entry mo. 82

86
100/**23 july 1958**
bayerischer rundfunk broadcast

lohengrin
bayreuth festival orchestra and chorus
conductor andré cluytens
chorus-master wilhelm pitz

lp: replica RPL 2489-2492
cd: myto MCD 89002
excerpts
lp: melodram MEL 085/MEL 590
cd: melodram MEL 37073

leonie rysanek (elsa)
astrid varnay (ortrud)
sandor konya (lohengrin)
kieth engen (könig heinrich)
ernest blanc (telramund)
eberhard wächter (heerrufer)
gerhard stolze (1.edler)
heinz-günther zimmermann (2.edler)
gotthard kronstein (3.edler)
egmont koch (4.edler)

bayerischer rundfunk states that it holds a second tape with the same cast but dated 3 august 1958

101/**24 july 1958**
bayerischer rundfunk broadcast

die meistersinger von nürnberg
bayreuth festival orchestra
and chorus
conductor andré cluytens
chorus-master wilhelm pitz

unpublished radio broadcast

elisabeth grümmer (eva)
elisabeth schärtel (magdalene)
josef traxel (stolzing)
gerhard stolze (david)
otto wiener (sachs)
hans hotter (pogner)
eberhard wächter (kothner)
karl schmitt-walter (beckmesser)
fritz uhl (vogelgesang)
egmont koch (nachtigall)
heinz-günther zimmermann (zorn)
erich benke (eisslinger)
hermann winkler (moser)
hans habietnik (ortel)
hans-günter nöcker (schwarz)
eugen fuchs (foltz)
donald bell (nachtwächter)

*bayerischer rundfunk states that
it holds a second tape with the same
cast but dated 2 august 1958*

102/**25 july 1958**
bayerischer rundfunk broadcast

parsifal
bayreuth festival orchestra
and chorus
conductor hans knappertsbusch
chorus-master wilhelm pitz

lp: melodram MEL 583
cd: golden melodram GM 10058

régine crespin (kundry)
hans beirer (parsifal)
eberhard wächter (amfortas)
jerome hines (gurnemanz)
toni blankenheim (klingsor)
josef greindl (titurel)
maria von ilosvay (stimme von oben)
lotte schädle (1.blumenmädchen)
friedl pöltinger (2.blumenmädchen)
hildegard schünermann (3.blumenmädchen)
dorothea siebert (4.blumenmädchen)
gertraud prenzlow (5.blumenmädchen)
elisabeth schärtel (6.blumenmädchen)
fritz uhl (1.gralsritter)
donald bell (2.gralsritter)
claudia hellmann (1.knappe)
ursula boese (2.knappe)
harald neukirch (3.knappe)
gerhard stolze (4.knappe)

103/**26 july 1958**
bayerischer rundfunk broadcast

tristan und isolde
bayreuth festival orchestra and chorus
conductor wolfgang sawallisch
chorus-master wilhelm pitz

unpublished radio broadcast

birgit nilsson (isolde)
grace hoffman (brangäne)
wolfgang windgassen (tristan)
erik saeden (kurwenal)
josef greindl (marke)
fritz uhl (melot)
hermann winkler (hirt)
egmont koch (steuermann)
josef traxel (ein junger seemann)

104/**27 july 1958**
bayerischer rundfunk broadcast

das rheingold
bayreuth festival orchestra
conductor hans knappertsbusch

lp: melodram MEL 586
cd: arkadia CDLSMH 34041/
    CDMP 441
cd: golden melodram GM 10052

hans hotter (wotan)
rita gorr (fricka)
elisabeth grümmer (freia)
maria von ilosvay (erda)
fritz uhl (loge)
sandor konya (froh)
gerhard stolze (mime)
erik saeden (donner)
frans andersson (alberich)
ludwig weber (fasolt)
josef greindl (fafner)
dorothea siebert (woglinde)
claudia hellmann (wellgunde)
ursula boese (flosshilde)

105/**28 july 1958**
bayerischer rundfunk broadcast

die walküre
bayreuth festival orchestra
conductor hans knappertsbusch

lp: melodram MEL 587
cd: arkadia CDLSMH 34042/
    CDMP 442
cd: golden melodram GM 10052
excerpts
cd: melodram MEL 37073

astrid varnay (brünnhilde)
leonie rysanek (sieglinde)
rita gorr (fricka and grimgerde)
jon vickers (siegmund)
hans hotter (wotan)
josef greindl (hunding)
marlies siemeling (gerhilde)
hilde scheppan (ortlinde)
elisabeth schärtel (waltraute)
maria von ilosvay (schwertleite)
lotte rysanek (helmwige)
grace hoffman (siegrune)
ursula boese (rossweisse)

106/30 july 1958
bayerischer rundfunk broadcast

siegfried
bayreuth festival orchestra
conductor hans knappertsbusch

lp: melodram MEL 588
cd: arkadia CDLSMH 34043/
 CDMP 443
cd: golden melodram GM 10052

astrid varnay (brünnhilde)
dorothea siebert (waldvogel)
maria von ilosvay (erda)
wolfgang windgassen (siegfried)
gerhard stolze (mime)
hans hotter (wanderer)
frans andersson (alberich)
josef greindl (fafner)

107/1 august 1958
bayerischer rundfunk broadcast

götterdämmerung
bayreuth festival orchestra and chorus
conductor hans knappertsbusch
chorus-master wilhelm pitz

lp: melodram MEL 589
cd: arkadia CDLSMH 34044/
 CDMP 444
cd: golden melodram GM 10052

astrid varnay (brünnhilde and 3.norn)
elisabeth grümmer (gutrune)
jean madeira (waltraute and 1.norn)
wolfgang windgassen (siegfried)
otto wiener (gunther)
josef greindl (hagen)
frans andersson (alberich)
dorothea siebert (woglinde)
claudia hellmann (wellgunde)
ursula boese (flosshilde and 2.norn)

108/22 august 1958
recordings made without audience by deutsche grammophon gesellschaft

der fliegende holländer: mit gewitter und sturm
bayreuth festival orchestra and chorus
conductor and chorus-master wilhelm pitz

45: deutsche grammophon EPL 30 426/SEPL 121 023
lp: deutsche grammophon LPEM 19 168/SLPEM 136 006/136 394/
    2535 180/2535 601
cd: deutsche grammophon 429 1692

der fliegende holländer: summ und brumm!
bayreuth festival orchestra and chorus
conductor and chorus-master wilhelm pitz

45: deutsche grammophon EPL 30 426/SEPL 121 023
lp: deutsche grammophon LPEM 19 168/SLPEM 136 006/136 388/
    136 394/2535 180/2535 645
cd: deutsche grammophon 429 1692

elisabeth schärtel (mary)

der fliegende holländer: steuermann lass die wacht!
bayreuth festival orchestra and chorus
conductor and chorus-master wilhelm pitz

45: deutsche grammophon EPL 30 426/SEPL 121 023
lp: deutsche grammophon LPEM 19 168/SLPEM 136 006/136 388/
    136 394/2535 180/2535 645
cd: deutsche grammophon 429 1692

22 august 1958/continued
tannhäuser: freudig begrüssen wir die edle halle (einzug der gäste); beglückt darf nun dich o heimat
bayreuth festival orchestra and chorus
conductor and chorus-master wilhelm pitz

45: deutsche grammophon EPL 30 427/SEPL 121 024
lp: deutsche grammophon LPEM 19 168/SLPEM 136 006/136 394/
    2535 180/2535 601
cd: deutsche grammophon 429 1692

tannhäuser: heil der gnade wunder!
bayreuth festival orchestra and chorus
conductor and chorus-master wilhelm pitz

45: deutsche grammophon EPL 30 427/SEPL 121 024
lp: deutsche grammophon LPEM 19 168/SPLEM 136 006/2535 180
cd: deutsche grammophon 429 1692

lohengrin: seht welch ein seltsam wunder!
bayreuth festival orchestra and chorus
conductor and chorus-master wilhelm pitz

lp: deutsche grammophon LPEM 19 168/SLPEM 136 006/2535 180
cd: deutsche grammophon 429 1692

lohengrin: gesegnet soll sie schreiten (zug zum münster)
bayreuth festival orchestra and chorus
conductor and chorus-master wilhelm pitz

lp: deutsche grammophon LPEM 19 168/SLPEM 136 006/2535 180/
    2535 631
cd: deutsche grammophon 429 1692

lohengrin: treulich geführt (brautchor)
bayreuth festival orchestra and chorus
conductor and chorus-master wilhelm pitz

45: deutsche grammophon EPL 30 426/SEPL 121 023
lp: deutsche grammophon LPEM 19 168/SLPEM 136 006/136 394/
    2535 180/2535 601
cd: deutsche grammophon 429 1692

22 august 1958/concluded
die meistersinger von nürnberg: wach auf! es nahet gen den tag; ehrt eure deutschen meister!
bayreuth festival orchestra and chorus
conductor and chorus-master wilhelm pitz

45: deutsche grammophon EPL 30 426/SEPL 121 023
lp: deutsche grammophon LPEM 19 168/SLPEM 136 006/2535 180
cd: deutsche grammophon 429 1692

götterdämmerung: hoiho ihr gibichsmannen!
bayreuth festival orchestra and chorus
conductor and chorus-master wilhelm pitz

lp: deutsche grammophon LPEM 19 168/SLPEM 136 006/2530 180
cd: deutsche grammophon 429 1692

josef greindl (hagen)

parsifal: zum letzten liebesmahle
bayreuth festival orchestra and chorus
conductor and chorus-master wilhelm pitz

lp: deutsche grammophon LPEM 19 168/SLPEM 136 006/136 394/
    2535 180/2535 645/411 2461/419 1141
cd: deutsche grammophon 429 1692

109/**23 july 1959**
bayerischer rundfunk broadcast

der fliegende holländer
bayreuth festival orchestra and chorus
conductor wolfgang sawallisch
chorus-master wilhelm pitz

lp: melodram MEL 590
cd: melodram MEL 26101
excerpts
lp: rodolphe RPC 12433-12434
lp: melodram MEL 650
cd: myto MCD 89002

leonie rysanek (senta)
res fischer (mary)
george london (holländer)
fritz uhl (erik)
georg paskuda (steuermann)
josef greindl (daland)

bayerischer rundfunk states that it holds a second tape with the same cast but dated 5 august 1959

110/**4 august 1959**
bayerischer rundfunk broiadcast

lohengrin
bayreuth festival orchestra and chorus
conductor lovro von matacic
chorus-master wilhelm pitz

lp: melodram MEL 591
cd: golden melodram GM 10002

elisabeth grümmer (elsa)
rita gorr (ortrud)
sandor konya (lohengrin)
franz crass (könig heinrich)
ernest blanc (telramund)
eberhard wächter (heerrufer)
harald neukirch (1.edler)
herold kraus (2.edler)
donald bell (3.edler)
hans-günter nöcker (4.edler)

rehearsal extracts were also preserved on film

111/6 august 1959
bayerischer rundfunk broadcast

die meistersinger von nürnberg
bayreuth festival orchestra and chorus
conductor erich leinsdorf
chorus-master wilhelm pitz
erich leinsdorf replaced otto klemperer as conductor

lp: melodram MEL 592
cd: golden melodram GM 10061

elisabeth grümmer (eva)
elisabeth schärtel (magdalene)
rudolf schock (stolzing)
gerhard stolze (david)
otto wiener (sachs)
josef greindl (pogner)
eberhard wächter (kothner)
toni blankenheim (beckmesser)
georg paskuda (vogelgesang)
egmont koch (nachtigall)
heinz-günther zimmermann (zorn)
harald neukirch (eisslinger)
hermann winkler (moser)
hans habietnik (ortel)
hans-günter nöcker (schwarz)
eugen fuchs (foltz)
donald bell (nachtwächter)

television recording was made of act one but probably not transmitted; rehearsal extracts were also preserved on film

112/**7 august 1959**
bayerischer rundfunk broadcast

parsifal
bayreuth festival orchestra and chorus
conductor hans knappertsbusch
chorus-master wilhelm pitz

cd: golden melodram GM 10070
act one as far as first scene with amfortas was inadvertently also published on cd by arkadia (CDKAR 219) and rca/bmg (74321 619502) in a vienna performance conducted by karajan; rca/bmg later corrected the error and substituted the actual vienna version

martha mödl (kundry)
hans beirer (parsifal)
eberhard wächter (amfortas)
jerome hines (gurnemanz)
toni blankenheim (klingsor)
josef greindl (titurel)
ursula boese (stimme von oben and 2.knappe)
ruth-margret pütz (1.blumenmädchen)
rita bartos (2.blumenmädchen)
gisela schröter (3.blumenmädchen)
dorothea siebert (4.blumenmädchen)
elisabeth witzmann (5.blumenmädchen)
claudia hellmann (6.blumenmädchen and 1.knappe)
georg paskuda (1.gralsritter)
donald bell (2.gralsritter)
harald neukirch (3.knappe)
herold kraus (4.knappe)

113/**8 august 1959**
bayerischer rundfunk broadcast

tristan und isolde
bayreuth festival orchestra
and chorus
conductor wolfgang sawallisch
chorus-master wilhelm pitz

unpublished radio broadcast

birgit nilsson (isolde)
grace hoffman (brangäne)
wolfgang windgassen (tristan)
frans andersson (kurwenal)
jerome hines (marke)
fritz uhl (melot)
hermann winkler (hirt)
donald bell (steuermann)
georg paskuda (ein junger seemann)

114/**23 july 1960**
bayerischer rundfunk broadcast

die meistersinger von nürnberg
bayreuth festival orchestra
and chorus
conductor hans knappertsbusch
chorus-master wilhelm pitz

lp: melodram MEL 602
cd: melodram MEL 46103
cd: golden melodram GM 10029

elisabeth grümmer (eva)
elisabeth schärtel (magdalene)
wolfgang windgassen (stolzing)
gerhard stolze (david)
josef greindl (sachs)
theo adam (pogner)
ludwig weber (kothner)
karl schmitt-walter (beckmesser)
wilfried krug (vogelgesang)
egmont koch (nachtigall)
heinz-günther zimmermann (zorn)
harald neukirch (eisslinger)
hermann winkler (moser)
fritjof sentpaul (ortel)
hans-günter nöcker (schwarz)
eugen fuchs (foltz)
donald bell (nachtwächter)

115/24 july 1960
bayerischer rundfunk broadcast

der fliegende holländer
bayreuth festival orchestra and chorus
conductor wolfgang sawallisch
chorus-master wilhelm pitz

unpublished radio broadcast

anja silja (senta)
res fischer (mary)
franz crass (holländer)
wolfgang windgassen (erik)
georg paskuda (steuermann)
josef greindl (daland)

116/25 july 1960
bayerischer rundfunk broadcast

lohengrin
bayreuth festival orchestra and chorus
conductor lorin maazel
chorus-master wilhelm pitz

lp: melodram MEL 601

aase nordmo-lövberg (elsa)
astrid varnay (ortrud)
wolfgang windgassen (lohengrin)
gustav neidlinger (telramund)
theo adam (könig heinrich)
eberhard wächter (heerrufer)
wilfried krug (1.edler)
hermann winkler (2.edler)
hans-günter nöcker (3.edler)
egmont koch (4.edler)

117/**26 july 1960**
bayerischer rundfunk broadcast

das rheingold
bayreuth festival orchestra
conductor rudolf kempe

lp: melodram MEL 606
cd: golden melodram GM 10027
cd: audiophile classics
 APL 101.846/APL 101.755

hermann uhde (wotan)
herta töpper (fricka)
ingrid bjoner (freia)
marga höffgen (erda)
gerhard stolze (loge)
georg paskuda (froh)
herold kraus (mime)
thomas stewart (donner)
otakar kraus (alberich)
peter roth-ehrang (fasolt)
arnold van mill (fafner)
dorothea siebert (woglinde)
claudia hellmann (wellgunde)
sona cervena (flosshilde)

118/**27 july 1960**
bayerischer rundfunk broadcast

die walküre
bayreuth festival orchestra
conductor rudolf kempe

lp: melodram MEL 607
cd: golden melodram GM 10027
cd: audiophile classics
 APL 101.846/APL 101.841

astrid varnay (brünnhilde)
aase nordmo-lövberg (sieglinde)
herta töpper (fricka)
wolfgang windgassen (siegmund)
jerome hines (wotan)
gottlob frick (hunding)
gertraud hopf (gerhilde)
frances martin (ortlinde)
claudia hellmann (waltraute)
rut siewert (schwertleite)
ingrid bjoner (helmwige)
grace hoffman (siegrune)
margit kobeck-peters (grimgerde)
dorothea von stein (rossweisse)

bayerischer rundfunk holds a second tape
of this performance in its archive dated
17 august 1960

119/**28 july 1960**
bayerischer rundfunk broadcast

siegfried
bayreuth festival orchestra
conductor rudolf kempe

lp: melodram MEL 608
cd: golden melodram GM 10027
cd: audiophile classics
    APL 101.846/APL 101.842

birgit nilsson (brünnhilde)
dorothea siebert (waldvogel)
marga höffgen (erda)
hans hopf (siegfried)
herold kraus (mime)
hermann uhde (wanderer)
otakar kraus (alberich)
peter roth-ehrang (fafner)

120/**30 july 1960**
bayerischer rundfunk broadcast

götterdämmerung
bayreuth festival orchestra and chorus
conductor rudolf kempe
chorus-master wilhelm pitz

lp: melodram MEL 609
cd: golden melodram GM 10027
cd: audiophile classics
    APL 101.846/APL 101.843

birgit nilsson (brünnhilde)
ingrid bjoner (gutrune)
grace hoffman (waltraute and 2.norn)
hans hopf (siegfried)
thomas stewart (gunther)
gottlob frick (hagen)
otakar kraus (alberich)
rut siewert (1.norn)
aase nordmo-lövberg (3.norn)
dorothea siebert (woglinde)
claudia hellmann (wellgunde)
sona cervena (flosshilde)

121/**31 july 1960**
bayerischer rundfunk broadcast

parsifal
bayreuth festival orchestra and chorus
conductor hans knappertsbusch
chorus-master wilhelm pitz

lp: melodram MEL 018/MEL 603
cd: gala GL 100.655
excerpts
lp: rodolphe RP 12445-12446
cd: rodolphe RPC 32445-32446

régine crespin (kundry)
hans beirer (parsifal)
thomas stewart (amfortas)
josef greindl (gurnemanz)
david ward (titurel)
gustav neidlinger (klingsor)
rut siewert (stimme von oben)
ruth-margret pütz (1.blumenmädchen)
gundula janowitz (2.blumenmädchen)
claudia hellmann (3.blumenmädchen and 1.knappe)
dorothea siebert (4.blumenmädchen)
elisabeth witzmann (5.blumenmädchen)
ruth hesse (6.blumenmädchen and 2.knappe)
wilfried krug (1.gralsritter)
theo adam (2.gralsritter)
harald neukirch (3.knappe)
herold kraus (4.knappe)

122/**23 july 1961**
bayerischer rundfunk broadcast

tannhäuser
bayreuth festival orchestra and chorus
conductor wolfgang sawallisch
chorus-master wilhelm pitz

lp: ed smith UORC 230
lp: teatro dischi (italy)
lp: melodram MEL 614
cd: myto MCD 93277

victoria de los angeles (elisabeth)
grace bumbry (venus)
wolfgang windgassen (tannhäuser)
josef greindl (landgraf)
dietrich fischer-dieskau (wolfram)
gerhard stolze (walter von der vogelweide)
franz crass (biterolf)
georg paskuda (heinrich der schreiber)
theo adam (reinmar von zweter)
else-margrete gardelli (ein junger hirt)

123/**24 july 1961**
bayerischer rundfunk broadcast

der fliegende holländer
bayreuth festival orchestra and chorus
conductor wolfgang sawallisch
chorus-master wilhelm pitz

unpublished radio broadcast

anja silja (senta)
res fischer (mary)
franz crass (holländer)
fritz uhl (erik)
josef greindl (daland)
georg paskuda (steuermann)

bayerischer rundfunk holds a second tape of this performance in its archive dated 31 july 1961

124/**25 july 1961**
bayerischer rundfunk broadcast

parsifal
bayreuth festival orchestra and chorus
conductor hans knappertsbusch
chorus-master wilhelm pitz

cd: golden melodram GM 10049
golden melodram issue dated august 1961

irene dalis (kundry)
jess thomas (parsifal)
george london (amfortas)
hans hotter (gurnemanz)
ludwig weber (titurel)
gustav neidlinger (klingsor)
ursula boese (stimme von oben)
gundula janowitz (1.blumenmädchen)
anja silja (2.blumenmädchen)
claudia hellmann (3.blumenmädchen and 1.knappe)
dorothea siebert (4.blumenmädchen)
rita bartos (5.blumenmädchen)
elisabeth schärtel (6.blumenmädchen)
niels moeller (1.gralsritter)
david ward (2.gralsritter)
ruth hesse (2.knappe)
gerhard stolze (3.knappe)
georg paskuda (4.knappe)

bayerischer rundfunk holds a second tape of this performance in its archive dated 5 august 1961

125/**26 july 1961**
bayerischer rundfunk broadcast

das rheingold
bayreuth festival orchestra
conductor rudolf kempe

unpublished radio broadcast

jerome hines (wotan)
regina resnik (fricka)
wilma schmidt (freia)
marga höffgen (erda)
gerhard stolze (loge)
david thaw (froh)
herold kraus (mime)
thomas stewart (donner)
otakar kraus (alberich)
david ward (fasolt)
peter roth-ehrang (fafner)
inga moussa-felderer (woglinde)
elisabeth steiner (wellgunde)
elisabeth schärtel (flosshilde)

126/**27 july 1961**
bayerischer rundfunk broadcast

die walküre
bayreuth festival orchestra
conductor rudolf kempe

cd: myto MCD 974164

astrid varnay (brünnhilde)
régine crespin (sieglinde)
regina resnik (fricka)
fritz uhl (siegmund)
jerome hines (wotan)
gottlob frick (hunding)
gertraud hopf (gerhilde)
wilma schmidt (ortlinde)
elisabeth schärtel (waltraute)
lilo brockhaus (schwertleite)
inga moussa-felderer (helmwige)
grace hoffman (siegrune)
elisabeth steiner (grimgerde)
ruth hesse (rossweisse)

127/**28 july 1961**
bayerischer rundfunk broadcast

siegfried
bayreuth festival orchestra
conductor rudolf kempe

unpublished radio broadcast

birgit nilsson (brünnhilde)
inga moussa-felderer (waldvogel)
marga höffgen (erda)
hans hopf (siegfried)
herold kraus (mime)
james milligan (wanderer)
otakar kraus (alberich)
peter roth-ehrang (fafner)

128/**30 july 1961**
bayerischer rundfunk broadcast

götterdämmerung
bayreuth festival orchestra and chorus
conductor rudolf kempe
chorus-master wilhelm pitz

unpublished radio broadcast

birgit nilsson (brünnhilde)
wilma schmidt (gutrune)
grace hoffman (waltraute and 2.norn)
hans hopf (siegfried)
thomas stewart (gunther)
gottlob frick (hagen)
otakar kraus (alberich)
elisabeth schärtel (1.norn and flosshilde)
régine crespin (3.norn)
inga moussa-felderer (woglinde)
elisabeth steiner (wellgunde)

129/**july-august 1961**
recording made by philips at performances betweeen 31 july and 18 august 1961

der fliegende holländer
bayreuth festival orchestra and chorus
conductor wolfgang sawallisch
chorus-master wilhelm pitz

lp: philips A02211-02213L/835 104-835 106AY/ABL 3412-3414/
    SABL 218-220/6723 001/6747 248
cd: philips 442 1032
excerpts
lp: philips 412 0241
lp: philips classical favourites G03092L/837 010GY/GL 5647/SGL 5647
lp: philips sequenza 6527 108

cast as for entry no. 123

130/**8 august 1961**
bayerischer rundfunk broadcast

die meistersinger von nürnberg
bayreuth festival orchestra and chorus
conductor josef krips
chorus-master wilhelm pitz

unpublished radio broadcast

elisabeth grümmer (eva)
elisabeth schärtel (magdalene)
wolfgang windgassen (stolzing)
gerhard stolze (david)
josef greindl (sachs)
theo adam (pogner)
ludwig weber (kothner)
karl schmitt-walter (beckmesser)
georg paskuda (vogelgesang)
egmont koch (nachtigall)
heinz-günther zimmermann (zorn)
harald neukirch (eisslinger)
hermann winkler (moser)
frithof sentpaul (ortel)
franz habietnik (schwarz)
eugen fuchs (foltz)
david ward (nachtwächter)

131/**24 july 1962**
bayerischer rundfunk broadcast

tristan und isolde
bayreuth festival orchestra and chorus
conductor karl böhm
chorus-master wilhelm pitz

lp: melodram MEL 625

birgit nilsson (isolde)
kerstin meyer (brangäne)
wolfgang windgassen (tristan)
eberhard wächter (kurwenal)
josef greindl (marke)
niels moeller (melot)
gerhard stolze (hirt)
hans-hanno daum (steuermann)
georg paskuda (ein junger seemann)

132/**july-august 1962**
recording made by philips at performances during july and august 1962

lohengrin
bayreuth festival orchestra and chorus
conductor wolfgang sawallisch
chorus-master wilhelm pitz

lp: philips 6747 241
cd: philips 446 3372
excerpts
lp: philips 412 0221
lp: philips sequenza 6527 108

anja silja (elsa)
astrid varnay (ortrud)
jess thomas (lohengrin)
ramon vinay (telramund)
franz crass (könig heinrich)
tom krause (heerrufer)
niels moeller (1.edler)
gerhard stolze (2.edler)
klaus kirchner (3.edler)
zoltan kelemen (4.edler)

133/**july-august 1962**
recording made by philips at performances during july and august 1962

tannhäuser
bayreuth festival orchestra and chorus
conductor wolfgang sawallisch
chorus-master wilhelm pitz

lp: philips A02303-02305L/835 178-835 180AY/AL 3445-3447/
    SAL 3445-3447/6723 001/6747 242/6747 249/6770 026
cd: philips 420 1222/434 4202/434 6072
excerpts
lp: philips 412 0231
lp: philips sequenza 6527 108
cd: philips 446 5102/446 6202

anja silja (elisabeth)
grace bumbry (venus)
wolfgang windgassen (tannhäuser)
eberhard wächter (wolfram)
josef greindl (landgraf)
gerhard stolze (walther von der vogelweide)
franz crass (biterolf)
georg paskuda (heinrich der schreiber)
gerd nienstedt (reinmar von zweter)
else-margrete gardelli (ein junger hirt)

134/**july-august 1962**
recording made by philips at performances during july and august 1962

parsifal
bayreuth festival orchestra and chorus
conductor hans knappertsbusch
chorus-master wilhelm pitz

lp: philips A02342-02346L/835 220-835 224AY/AL 3475-3479/
    SAL 3475-3479/6723 001/6747 242/6747 250
lp: philips (usa) PHM 5550/PHS 5950
cd: philips 416 3902/464 7562

martti talvela (titurel)
ursula boese (stimme von oben and 2.knappe)
else-margrete gardelli (3.blumenmädchen)
sona cervena (6.blumenmädchen and 1.knappe)
gerd nienstedt (2.gralsritter)
rest of cast as for entry no. 124

135/**28 july 1962**
bayerischer rundfunk broadcast

das rheingold
bayreuth festival orchestra
conductor rudolf kempe

unpublished radio broadcast

otto wiener (wotan)
grace hoffman (fricka)
jutta meyfarth (freia)
marga höffgen (erda)
horst wilhelm (froh)
gerhard stolze (loge)
erich kraus (mime)
otakar kraus (alberich)
walter kreppel (fasolt)
peter roth-ehrang (fafner)
gundula janowitz (woglinde)
elisabeth schwarzenberg (wellgunde)
sieglinde wagner (flosshilde)

136/**29 july 1962**
bayerischer rundfunk broadcast

die walküre
bayreuth festival orchestra
conductor rudolf kempe

unpublished radio broadcast

astrid varnay (brünnhilde)
jutta meyfarth (sieglinde)
grace hoffman (fricka and siegrune)
fritz uhl (siegmund)
otto wiener (woran)
gottlob frick (hagen)
gertraud hopf (gerhilde)
elisabeth schwarzenberg (ortlinde)
anni argy (waltraute)
erika schubert (schwertleite)
ingeborg moussa-felderer (helmwige)
sieglinde wagner (grimgerde)
margarete bence (rossweisse)

137/**30 july 1962**
bayerischer rundfunk broadcast

siegfried
bayreuth festival orchestra
conductor rudolf kempe

unpublished radio broadcast

birgit nilsson (brünnhilde)
ingeborg moussa-felderer (waldvogel)
marga höffgen (erda)
hans hopf (siegfried)
erich kraus (mime)
otto wiener (wanderer)
peter roth-ehrang (fafner)
otakar kraus (alberich)

138/**1 august 1962**
bayerischer rundfunk broadcast

götterdämmerung
bayreuth festival orchestra and chorus
conductor rudolf kempe
chorus-master wilhelm pitz

unpublished radio broadcast

birgit nilsson (brünnhilde)
jutta meyfarth (gutrune)
margarete bence (waltraute)
hans hopf (siegfried)
marcel cordes (gunther)
gottlob frick (hagen)
otakar kraus (alberich)
elisabeth schärtel (1.norn)
grace hoffman (2.norn)
gertraud hopf (3.norn)
gundula janowitz (woglinde)
elisabeth schwarzenberg (wellgunde)
sieglinde wagner (flosshilde)

139/2 august 1962
bayerischer rundfunk broadcast: first live stereo broadcast from bayreuth

tannhäuser
bayreuth festival orchestra and chorus
conductor wolfgang sawallisch
chorus-master wilhelm pitz

unpublished radio broadcast

cast as for entry no. 133

bayerischer rundfunk states that it has a second tape in its archive dated 7 august 1962

140/3 august 1962
bayerischer rundfunk broadcast

lohengrin
bayreuth festival orchestra and chorus
conductor wolfgang sawallisch
chorus-master wilhelm pitz

unpublished radio broadcast

cast as for entry no. 132

141/5 august 1962
bayerischer rundfunk broadcasat

parsifal
bayreuth festival orchestra and chorus
conductor hans knappertsbusch
chorus-master wilhelm pitz

unpublished radio broadcast

cast as for entry no. 134

142/**23 july 1963**
bayerischer rundfunk recording

beethoven: symphony no 9 "choral"
bayreuth festival orchestra and chorus
conductor karl böhm
chorus-master wilhelm pitz

lp: melodram MEL 650
cd: melodram MEL 18005
an unsatisfactory CD issue on the classical collection label contained only three of the symphony's four movements

gundula janowitz
grace bumbry
jess thomas
george london

143/**24 july 1963**
bayerischer rundfunk broadcast

parsifal
bayreuth festival orchestra and chorus
conductor hans knappertsbusch
chorus-master wilhelm pitz

cd: golden melodram GM 10034

irene dalis (kundry)
george london (amfortas)
jess thomas (parsifal)
hans hotter (gurnemanz)
heinz hagenau (titurel)
gustav neidlinger (klingsor)
ruth hesse (stimme von oben and 1.knappe)
sylvia stahlman (1.blumenmädchen)
anja silja (2.blumenmädchen)
sieglinde wagner (3.blumenmädchen)
dorothea siebert (4.blumenmädchen)
rita bartos (5.blumenmädchen)
sona cervena (6.blumenmädchen)
hermann winkler (1.gralsritter)
gerd nienstedt (2.gralsritter)
margarete bence (2.knappe)
georg paskuda (3.knappe)
erwin wohlfahrt (4.knappe)

144/ **25 july 1963**
bayerischer rundfunk broadcast

die meistersinger von nürnberg
bayreuth festival orchestra
and chorus
conductor thomas schippers
chorus-master wilhelm pitz

unpublished radio broadcast and
unpublished video recording of
rehearsal extracts

anja silja (eva)
ruth hesse (magdalene)
jess thomas (stolzing)
erwin wohlfahrt (david)
otto wiener (sachs)
kurt böhme (pogner)
gustav neidlinger (kothner)
carlos alexander (beckmesser)
ticho parly (nachtigall)
stefan schwer (zorn)
günther treptow (eisslinger)
hermann winkler (moser)
zoltan kelemen (ortel)
fritz linke (schwarz)
ernst krukowski (foltz)
heinz hagenau (nachtwächter)

bayerischer rundfunk states that it has
a second tape in its archive dated
2 august 1963

*145//*26 july 1963
bayerischer rundfunk broadcast

tristan und isolde
bayreuth festival orchestra
and chorus
conductor karl böhm
chorus-master wilhelm pitz

unpublished radio broadcast

birgit nilsson (isolde)
kerstin meyer (brangäne)
wolfgang windgassen (tristan)
eberhard wächter (kurwenal)
josef greindl (marke)
niels moeller (melot)
gerhard stolze (hirt)
hans-hanno daum (steuermann)
georg paskuda (junger seemann)

146/**27 july 1963**
bayerischer rundfunk broadcast

das rheingold
bayreuth festival orchestra
conductor rudolf kempe

unpublished radio broadcast

theo adam (wotan)
grace hoffman (fricka)
jutta meyfarth (freia)
marcel cordes (donner)
horst wilhelm (froh)
ken neate (loge)
otakar kraus (alberich)
franz crass (fasolt)
peter roth-ehrang (fafner)
marga höffgen (erda)
barbara holt (woglinde)
sieglinde wagner (wellgunde)
elisabeth schwarzenberg (flosshilde)

147/**28 july 1963**
bayerischer rundfunk broadcast

die walküre
bayreuth festival orchestra
conductor rudolf kempe

unpublished radio broadcast

anita välkki (brünnhilde)
jutta meyfarth (sieglinde)
grace hoffman (fricka and siegrune)
fritz uhl (siegmund)
hans hotter (wotan)
gottlob frick (hunding)
gertraud hopf (gerhilde)
elisabeth schwarzenberg (ortlinde)
elisabeth schärtel (waltraute)
ruth hesse (schwertleite)
inga moussa-felderer (helmwige)
sieglinde wagner (grimgerde)
margarete bence (rossweisse)

148/**29 july 1963**
bayerischer rundfunk broadcast

siegfried
bayreuth festival orchestra
conductor rudolf kempe

unpublished radio broadcast

astrid varnay (brünnhilde)
marga höffgen (erda)
barbara holt (waldvogel)
hans hopf (siegfried)
otto wiener (wanderer)
erich klaus (mime)
otakar kraus (alberich)
peter roth-ehrang (fafner)

149/**31 july 1963**
bayerischer rundfunk broadcast

götterdämmerung
bayreuth festival orchestra and chorus
conductor rudolf kempe
chorus-master wilhelm pitz

unpublished radio broadcast

astrid varnay (brünnhilde)
jutta meyfarth (gutrune)
elisabeth schärtel (waltraute and 1.norn)
hans hopf (siegfried)
marcel cordes (gunther)
gottlob frick (hagen)
otakar kraus (alberich)
grace hoffman (2.norn)
anita välkki (3.norn)
barbara holt (woglinde)
elisabeth schwarzenberg (wellgunde)
sieglinde wagner (flosshilde)

bayerischer rundfunk states that it holds
a second tape in its archive dated
15 august 1963 (role of waltraute
taken by margarete bence)

150/**18 august 1963**
bayerisches fernsehen

die meistersinger von nürnberg: ein werbelied von sachs?...so ganz boshaft doch keinen ich fand
bayreuth festival orchestra
conductor thomas schippers

unpublished video recording
first televised extract from a performance in the bayreuth festspielhaus

josef greindl (sachs)
carlos alexander (beckmesser)

151/**18 july 1964**
bayerischer rundfunk broadcast

tristan und isolde
bayreuth festival orchestra and chorus
conductor karl böhm
chorus-master wilhelm pitz

unpublished radio broadcast

cast as for entry no. 145

152/**19 july 1964**
bayerischer rundfunk broadcast

tannhäuser
bayreuth festival orchestra and chorus
conductor otmar suitner
chorus-master wilhelm pitz
otmar suitner replaced carlo maria giulini as conductor

cd: golden melodram GM 10050

leonie rysanek (elisabeth)
barbro ericson (venus)
wolfgang windgassen (tannhäuser)
eberhard wächter (wolfram)
martti talvela (landgraf)
arturo sergi (walther von der vogelweide)
hubert hofmann (biterolf)
hermann winkler (heinrich der schreiber)
gerd nienstedt (reinmar von zweter)
else-margrete gardelli (ein junger hirt)

153/20 july 1964
bayerischer rundfunk broadcast

die meistersinger von nürnberg

bayreuth festival orchestra
and chorus
conductor karl böhm
chorus-master wilhelm pitz

cd: golden melodram GM 10074

anja silja (eva)
ruth hesse (magdalene)
sandor konya (stolzing)
erwin wohlfahrt (david)
josef greindl (sachs)
kurt böhme (pogner)
carlos alexander (beckmesser)
ticho parly (vigelgesang)
gustav neidlinger (kothner)
stefan schwer (zorn)
günther treptow (eisslinger)
hermann winkler (moser)
zoltan kelemen (ortel)
fritz linke (schwarz)
ralph telasco (foltz)
heinz hagenau (nachtwächter)

154/21 july 1964
bayerischer rundfunk broadcast

parsifal

bayreuth festival orchestra and chorus
conductor hans knappertsbusch
chorus-master wilhelm pitz
final bayreuth season of hans knappertsbusch
as conductor of parsifal

lp: melodram MEL 643
cd: arkadia CDLSMH 34051/
        CDMP 451
cd: golden melodram GM 10004
golden melodram edition published in
collaboration with hans-knappertsbusch-
gesellschaft: it claims to be the actual final
public performance by knappertsbusch on
13 august 1964, of which bayerischer
rundfink also states it holds a tape in its
archive

jon vickers (parsifal)
barbro ericson (kundry)
thomas stewart (amfortas)
hans hotter (gurnemanz)
heinz hagenau (titurel)
gustav neidlinger (klingsor)
ruth hesse (stimme von oben and 1.knappe)
anja silja (1.blumenmädchen)
liselotte rebmann (2.blumenmädchen)
else-margrete gardelli (3.blumenmädchen)
dorothea siebert (4.blumnmädchen)
rita bartos (5.blumenmädchen)
sylvia lindenstrand (6.blumenmädchen and 2.knappe)
hermann winkler (1.gralsritter)
gerd nienstedt (2.gralsritter)
dieter slembeck (3.knappe)
erwin wohlfahrt (4.knappe)

155/**22 july 1964**
bayerischer rundfunk broadcast

das rheingold
bayreuth festival orchestra
conductor berislav klobucar

unpublished radio broadcast

theo adam (wotan)
grace hoffman (fricka)
jutta meyfarth (freia)
marga höffgen (erda)
hans hopf (froh)
gerhard stolze (loge)
erich kraus (mime)
zoltan kelemen (alberich)
gottlob frick (fasolt)
peter roth-ehrang (fafner)
barbara holt (woglinde)
sieglinde wagner (wellgunde)
elisabeth schwarzenberg (flosshilde)

156/**23 july 1964**
bayerischer rundfunk broadcast

die walküre
bayreuth festival orchestra
conductor berislav klobucar

unpublished radio broadcast

anita välkki (brünnhilde)
jutta meyfarth (sieglinde)
grace hoffman (fricka and siegrune)
theo adam (wotan)
fritz uhl (siegmund)
gottlob frick (hunding)
gertraud hopf (gerhilde)
elisabeth schwarzenberg (ortlinde)
ursula freudenberg (waltraute)
maria von ilosvay (schwertleite)
eva-maria kupczyk (helmwigre)
sieglinde wagner (grimgerde)
erika schubert (rossweisse)

157/**24 july 1964**
bayerischer rundfunk broadcast

siegfried
bayreuth festival orchestra
conductor berislav klobucar

unpublished radio broadcast

astrid varnay (brünnhilde)
barbara holt (waldvogel)
marga höffgen (erda)
hans hopf (siegfried)
erich kraus (mime)
hubert hofmann (wanderer)
zoltan kelemen (alnerich)
peter roth-ehrang (fafner)

158/**26 july 1964**
bayerischer rundfunk broadcast

götterdämmerung
bayreuth festival orchestra and chorus
conductor berislav klobucar
chorus-master wilhelm pitz

unpublished radio broadcast

astrid varnay (brünnhilde)
jutta meyfarth (gutrune)
grace hoffman (waltraute and 2.norn)
hans hopf (siegfried)
marcel cordes (gunther)
gottlob frick (hagen)
zoltan kelemen (alberich)
marga höffgen (1.norn)
anita välkki (3.norn)
barbara holt (woglinde)
elisabeth schwarzenberg (wellgunde)
sieglinde wagner (flosshilde)

159/**25 july 1965**
bayerischer rundfunk broadcast

das rheingold
bayreuth festival orchestra
conductor karl böhm

lp: golden treasury (usa) GTR 1

theo adam (wotan)
ursula boese (fricka)
anja silja (freia)
lili chookasian (erda)
william olvis (froh)
wolfgang windgassen (loge)
erwin wohlfahrt (mime)
gerd nienstedt (donner)
gustav neidlinger (alberich)
martti talvela (fasolt)
kurt böhme (fafner)
dorothea siebert (woglinde)
helga dernesch (wellgunde)
kerstin meyer (flosshilde)

160/**26 july 1965**
bayerischer rundfunk broadcast

die walküre
bayreuth festival orchestra
conductor karl böhm

unpublished radio broadcast
excerpts
cd: legato SRO 833

birgit nilsson (brünnhilde)
leonie rysanek (sieglinde)
ursula boese (fricka and grimgerde)
theo adam (wotan)
james king (siegmund)
martti talvela (hunding)
danica mastilovic (gerhilde)
isabella doran (ortlinde)
gertraud hopf (waltraute)
lili chookasian (schwertleite)
liane synek (helmwige)
elisabeth schärtel (siegrune)
margarete bence (rossweisse)

161/**28 july 1965**
bayerischer rundfunk broadcast

siegfried
bayreuth festival orchestra
conductor karl böhm

unpublished radio broadcast

birgit nilsson (brünnhilde)
erika köth (waldvogel)
lili chookasian (erda)
wolfgang windgassen (siegfried)
erwin wohlfahrt (mime)
josef greindl (wanderer)
gustav neidlinger (alberich)
kurt böhme (fafner)

162/**30 july 1965**
bayerischer rundfunk broadcast

götterdämmerung
bayreuth festival orchestra and chorus
conductor karl böhm
chorus-master wilhelm pitz

unpublished radio broadcast

birgit nilsson (brünnhilde)
ludmila dvorakova (gutrune)
kerstin meyer (waltraute and flosshilde)
wolfgang windgassen (siegfried)
thomas stewart (gunther)
josef greindl (hagen)
gustav neidlinger (alberich)
lili chookasian (1.norn)
ursula boese (2.norn)
anja silja (3.norn)
dorothea siebert (woglinde)
helga dernesch (wellgunde)

rehearsal extracts from the 1965 ring cycle were included in the tv documentary
wieland wagner probt den ring/ ein film von werner lütje

163/**9 august 1965**
bayerischer rundfunk broadcast

tannhäuser
bayreuth festival orchestra and chorus
conductor andré cluytens
chorus-master wilhelm pitz

unpublished radio broadcast

leonie rysanek (elisabeth)
ludmila dvorakova (venus)
wolfgang windgassen (tannhäuser)
hermann prey (wolfram von eschenbach)
martti talvela (landgraf)
willy hartmann (walther von der vogelweide)
gerd nienstedt (biterolf)
hermann winkler (heinrich der schreiber)
dieter slembeck (reinmar von zweter)
oliviera miljakovic (ein junger hirt)

164/**10 august 1965**
bayerischer rundfunk broadcast

parsifal
bayreuth festival orchestra
and chorus
conductor andré cluytens
chorus-master wilhelm pitz

unpublished radio broadcast

astrid varnay (kundry)
jess thomas (parsifal)
theo adam (amfortas)
hans hotter (gurnemanz)
martti talvela (titurel)
gustav neidlinger (klingsor)
ruth hesse (stimme von oben and
    1.knappe)
anja silja (1.blumenmädchen)
simone mangelsdorff (2.blumenmädchen)
helga dernesch (3.blumenmädchen)
dorothea siebert (4.blumenmädchen)
rita bartos (5.blumenmädchen)
elisabeth schärtel (6.blumenmädchen
    and 2.knappe)
hermann winkler (1.gralsritter)
gerd nienstedt (2.gralsritter)
dieter slembeck (3.knappe)
erwin wohlfahrt (4.knappe)

165/**11 august 1965**
bayerischer rundfunk broadcast

der fliegende holländer
bayreuth festival orchestra
and chorus
conductor otmar suitner
chorus-master wilhelm pitz

unpublished radio broadcast

anja silja (senta)
lili chookasian (mary)
thomas stewart (holländer)
william olvis (erik)
hermann winkler (steuermann)
josef greindl (daland)

166/**july-august 1966**
recorded by philips at rehearsals between 14-16 july and at performances on 4 and 16 august: decision to publish the recording on the deutsche grammophon label was taken at a later date

tristan und isolde
bayreuth festival orchestra and chorus
conductor karl böhm
chorus-master wilhelm pitz

lp: deutsche grammophon KL 512-516/SKL 912-916/LPM 39 221-39 225/ SLPM 139 221-139 225/2713 001/2740 144/415 3951
lp: philips 6747 243
lp: supraphon 112 0891-112 0895
cd: deutsche grammophon 419 8992/449 7722
cd: philips 434 4202/434 4252
excerpts
lp: deutsche grammophon 135 118/136 433/2535 243/2536 037/2537 001/ 2538 098/2538 245/2705 015/2721 112/2721 115/410 8551/424 3471
lp: philips 6833 195
lp: supraphon 111 93751-93752
lp: metropolitan opera MET 506
cd: deutsche grammophon 424 8672/439 4692
cd: philips 446 6172
rehearsal extracts
lp: deutsche grammophon KL 512-516/SKL 912-916/LPM 39 221-39 225/ SLPM 139 221-139 225
lp: philips 6701 048

birgit nilsson (isolde)
christa ludwig (brangäne)
wolfgang windgassen (tristan)
eberhard wächter (kurwenal)
martti talvela (marke)
claude heater (melot)
erwin wohlfahrt (hirt)
gerd nienstedt (steuermann)
peter schreier (ein junger seemann)

167/**24 july 1966**
bayerischer rundfunk broadcast

tannhäuser
bayreuth festival orchestra
and chorus
conductor carl melles
chorus-master wilhelm pitz

cd: golden melodram GM 10033

leonie rysanek (elisabeth)
ludmilla dvorakova (venus)
jess thomas (tannhäuser)
hermann prey (wolfram)
martti talvela (landgraf)
willy hartmann (walther von der vogelweide)
gerd nienstedt (biterolf)
hermann winkler (heinrich der schreiber)
dieter slembeck (reinmar von zweter)
oliviera miljakovic (ein junger hirt)

168/**25 july 1966**
bayerischer rundfunk broadcast

parsifal
bayreuth festival orchestra
and chorus
conductor pierre boulez
chorus-master wilhelm pitz

cd: golden melodram GM 10037

astrid varnay (kundry)
sandor konya (parsifal)
eberhard wächter (amfortas)
josef greindl (gurnemanz)
kurt böhme (titurel)
gustav neidlinger (klingsor)
ruth hesse (stimme von oben und 1.knappe)
anja silja (1.blumenmädchen)
lily sauter (2.blumenmädchen)
helga dernesch (3.blumenmädchen)
dorothea siebert (4.blumenmädchen)
rita bartos (5.blumenmädchen)
sona cervena (6.blumenmädchen)
hermann winkler (1.gralsritter)
gerd nienstedt (2.gralsritter)
elisabeth schärtel (2.knappe)
dieter slembeck (3.knappe)
erwin wohlfahrt (4.knappe)

169/**26 july 1966**
philips recording and bayerischer rundfunk broadcast

das rheingold
bayreuth festival orchestra
conductor karl böhm

lp: philips 6747 037/6747 046
cd: philips 412 4752/420 3252/
    446 0572/464 7512
excerpts
lp: philips 6575 500/6575 504
cd: philips 454 0202
446 0572 is incorrectly dated 1967

theo adam (wotan)
annelies burmeister (fricka)
anja silja (freia)
vera soukupova (erda)
gerd nienstedt (donner)
hermin esser (froh)
wolfgang windgassen (loge)
erwin wohlfahrt (mime)
gustav neidlinger (alberich)
martti talvela (fasolt)
kurt böhme (fafner)
dorothea siebert (woglinde)
helga dernesch (wellgunde)
ruth hesse (flosshilde)

170/**27 july 1966**
bayerischer rundfunk broadcast

die walküre
bayreuth festival orchestra
conductor karl böhm

unpublished radio broadcast

birgit nilsson (brünnhilde)
leonie rysanek (sieglinde)
annelies burmeister (fricka and siegrune)
james king (siegmund)
theo adam (wotan)
martti talvela (hunding)
danica mastilovic (gerhilde)
helga dernesch (ortlinde)
gertraud hopf (waltraute)
ruth hesse (schwertleite)
liane synek (helmwige)
elisabeth schärtel (grimgerde)
sona cervena (rossweisse)

171/**29 july 1966**
philips recording and bayerischer rundfunk broadcast

siegfried
bayreuth festival orchestra
conductor karl böhm

lp: philips 6747 037/6747 048
cd: philips 412 4832.420 3252/
   446 0572
excerpts
lp: philips 6575 502/6575 504
cd: philips 454 0202
446 0572 is incorrectly dated 1967

birgit nilsson (brünnhilde)
vera soukupova (erda)
erika köth (waldvogel)
wolfgang windgassen (siegfried)
theo adam (wanderer)
erwin wohlfahrt (mime)
gustav neidlinger (alberich)
kurt böhme (fafner)

172/**31 july 1966**
bayerischer rundfunk broadcast

götterdämmerung
bayreuth festival orchestra and chorus
conductor karl böhm
chorus-master wilhelm pitz

unpublished radio broadcast

birgit nilsson (brünnhilde)
ludmila dvorakova (gutrune)
martha mödl (waltraute)
wolfgang windgassen (siegfried)
thomas stewart (gunther)
josef greindl (hagen)
gustav neidlinger (alberich)
vera soukupova (1.norn)
elsa cavelti (2.norn)
anja silja (3.norn)
dorothea siebert (woglinde)
helga dernesch (wellgunde)
ruth hesse (flosshilde)

173/**4 august 1966**
bayerischer rundfunk broadcast

tristan und isolde
bayreuth festival orchestra and chorus
conductor karl böhm
chorus-master wilhelm pitz

cd: frequenz CML 3
cd: movimento musica 051.051
excerpts
cd: memories HR 4275-4276/HR 4424-4425
cd: curcio OPV 16
all issues incorrectly dated 13 august 1966

cast as for entry no. 166

174/**17 october 1966**
bayerischer rundfunk recording of memorial service for wieland wagner

bach matthäus-passion: wir setzen uns mit tränen nieder
bayreuth festival orchestra and chorus
conductor pierre boulez
chorus-master wilhelm pitz

unpublished radio broadcast

175/**10 april 1967/osaka festival hall**
japanese television recording of a guest performance by the bayreuth festival

tristan und isolde
nhk symphony orchestra and chorus
conductor pierre boulez

vhs video: legato classics LCV 005
vhs video: bel canto society BCS 0462

birgit nilsson (isolde)
herta töpper (brangäne)
wolfgang windgassen (tristan)
frans andersson (kurwenal)
hans hotter (marke)
gerd nienstedt (melot and steuermann)
sebastian feiersinger (hirt)
georg paskuda (ein junger seemann)

176/**april 1967/osaka festival hall**
japanese television recording of a guest performance by the bayreuth festival

die walküre
nhk symphony orchestra
conductor thomas schippers

unpublished video recording
videotape believed to be in the possession of anja silja
excerpts
lp: legendary recordings LR 131

anja silja (brünnhilde)
helga dernesch (sieglinde)
grace hoffman (fricka)
jess thomas (siegmund)
theo adam (wotan)
gerd nienstedt (hunding)

these japanese recordings remain the sole extant visual documentation of
complete stage productions by wieland wagner

177/**21 july 1967**
bayerischer rundfunk broadcast

lohengrin
bayreuth festival orchestra and chorus
conductor rudolf kempe
chorus-master wilhelm pitz

cd: golden melodram GM 10035
golden melodram issue is dated 28 july 1967

sandor konya (lohengrin)
heather harper (elsa)
grace hoffman (ortrud)
donald mcintyre (telramund)
karl ridderbusch (könig heinrich)
thomas tipton (heerrufer)
horst hoffman (1.edler)
hermin esser (2.edler)
dieter slembeck (3.edler)
heinz feldhoff (4.edler)

bayerischer rundfunk states that it holds a second tape in its archive dated 30 july 1967

178/**22 july 1967**
bayerischer rundfunk broadcast

das rheingold
bayreuth festival orchestra
conductor otmar suitner

unpublished radio broadcast

thomas stewart (wotan)
annelies burmeister (fricka)
anja silja (freia)
marga höffgen (erda)
gerd nienstedt (donner)
hermin esser (froh)
wolfgang windgassen (loge)
erwin wohlfahrt (mime)
gustav neidlinger (alberich)
karl ridderbusch (fasolt)
kurt böhme (fafner)
dorothea siebert (woglinde)
helga dernesch (wellgunde)
sieglinde wagner (flosshilde)

179/**23 july 1967**
bayerischer rundfunk broadcast

die walküre
bayreuth festival orchestra
conductor otmar suitner

unpublished radio broadcast

ludmila dvorakova (brünnhilde)
leonie rysanek (sieglinde)
martha mödl (fricka)
james king (siegmund)
thomas stewart (wotan)
josef greindl (hunding)
danica mastilovic (gerhilde)
helga dernesch (ortlinde)
gertraud hopf (waltraute)
sieglinde wagner (schwertleite)
liane synek (helmwige)
annelies burmeister (siegrune)
elisabeth schärtel (grimgerde)
sona cervena (rossweisse)

180/**25 july 1967**
bayerischer rundfunk broadcast

siegfried
bayreuth festival orchestra
conductor otmar suitner

unpublished radio broadcast

ludmila dvorakova (brünnhilde)
marga höffgen (erda)
anja silja (waldvogel)
wolfgang windgassen (siegfried)
josef greindl (wanderer)
erwin wohlfahrt (mime)
gustav neidlinger (alberich)
kurt böhme (fafner)

181/**27 july 1967**
bayerischer rundfunk broadcast and philips recording at this performance and further ones in august 1967

götterdämmerung
bayreuth festival orchestra and chorus
conductor karl böhm
chorus-master wilhelm pitz

lp: philips 6747 037/6747 049
cd: philips 412 4882/420 3252/
     446 0572
excerpts
lp: philips 6575 303/6575 504/
     6833 083
cd: philips 454 0202

birgit nilsson (brünnhilde)
ludmila dvorakova (gutrune)
martha mödl (waltraute)
wolfgang windgassen (siegfried)
thomas stewart (gunther)
josef greindl (hagen)
gustav beidlinger (alberich)
marga höffgen (1.norn)
annelies burmeister (2.norn)
anja silja (3.norn)
dorothea siebert (woglinde)
helga dernesch (wellgunde)
sieglinde wagner (flosshilde)

182/**28 july 1967**
bayerischer rundfunk broadcast

parsifal
bayreuth festival orchestra
and chorus
conductor pierre boulez
chorus-master wilhelm pitz

unpublished radio broadcast

christa ludwig (kundry)
james king (parsifal)
thomas stewart (amfortas)
franz crass (gurnemanz)
karl ridderbusch (titurel)
gerd nienstedt (klingsor)
martha mödl (stimme von oben)
anja silja (1.blumenmädchen)
dorothea siebert (2.blumenmädchen)
lily sauter (3.blumenmädchen)
rita bartos (4.blumenmädchen)
helga dernesch (5.blumenmädchen)
sona cervena (6.blumenmädchen)
hermin esser (1.gralsritter)
kurt moll (2.gralsritter)
elisabeth schärtel (1.knappe)
annelies burmeister (2.knappe)
dieter slembeck (3.knappe)
horst hoffman (4.knappe)

183/**29 july 1967**
bayerischer rundfunk broadcast

tannhäuser
bayreuth festival orchestra
and chorus
conductor berislav klobucar
chorus-master wilhelm pitz
berislav klobucar replaced christoph von dodnanyi as conductor

unpublished radio broadcast

anja silja (elisabeth)
berit lindholm (venus)
jess thomas (tannhäuser)
hermann prey (wolfram)
tugomir franc (landgraf)
hermin esser (walther von der vogelweide)
gerd nienstedt (biterolf)
horst hoffman (heinrich der schreiber)
dieter slembeck (reinmar von zweter)
lily sauter (ein junger hirt)

184/ **august 1967**
recorded by philips at performances during august

die walküre
bayreuth festival orchestra
conductor karl böhm

lp: philips 6747 037/6747 047
cd: philips 412 4782/420 3252/446 0572
excerpts
lp: philips 6575 501/6575 504/6833 083
cd: philips 454 0202

birgit nilsson (brünnhilde)
leonie rysanek (sieglinde)
annelies burmeister (fricka and siegrune)
james king (siegmund)
theo adam (wotan)
gerd nienstedt (hunding)
danica mastilovic (gerhilde)
helga dernesch (ortlinde)
gertraud hopf (waltraute)
sieglinde wagner (schwertleite)
liane synek (helmwige)
elisabeth schärtel (grimgerde)
sona cervena (rossweisse)

185/**25 july 1968**
bayerischer rundfunk broadcast

die meistersinger von nürnberg
bayreuth festival orchestra
and chorus
conductor karl böhm
chorus-master wilhelm pitz

cd: golden melodram GM 10038
golden melodram incorrectly dated 1969

gwyneth jones (eva)
janis martin (magdalene)
waldemar kmentt (stolzing)
hermin esser (david)
theo adam (sachs)
karl ridderbusch (pogner)
gerd nienstedt (kothner)
thomas hemsley (beckmesser)
sebastian feiersinger (vogelgesang)
dieter slembeck (nachtigall)
günther treptow (zorn)
erich klaus (eisslinger)
william johns (moser)
heinz feldhoff (ortel)
fritz linke (schwarz)
hans frantzen (foltz)
kurt moll (nachtwächter)

186/**26 july 1968**
bayerischer rundfunk recording

lohengrin
bayreuth festival orchestra and chorus
conductor alberto erede
chorus-master wilhelm pitz

unpublished radio broadcast

heather harper (elsa)
ludmila dvorakova (ortrud)
james king (lohengrin)
donald mcintyre (telramund)
karl ridderbusch (könig heinrich)
thomas stewart (heerrufer)
horst hoffmann (1.edler)
william johns (2.edler)
dieter slembeck (3.edler)
heinz feldhoff (4.edler)

187/**27 july 1968**
bayerischer rundfunk recording

parsifal
bayreuth festival orchestra
and chorus
conductor pierre boulez
chorus-master wilhelm pitz

unpublished radio broadcast

amy shuard (kundry)
jean cox (parsifal)
thomas stewart (amfortas)
franz crass (gurnemanz)
karl ridderbusch (titurel)
donald mcintyre (klingsor)
unni rugtvedt (stimme von oben)
hannelore bode (1.blumenmädchen)
lily sauter (2.blumenmädchen)
helga dernesch (3.blumenmädchen)
dorothea siebert (4.blumenmädchen)
wendy fine (5.blumenmädchen)
sieglinde wagner (6.blumenmädchen and
   2.knappe)
hermin esser (1.gralsritter)
kurt moll (2.gralsritter)
elisabeth schwarzenberg (1.knappe)
dieter slembeck (3.knappe)
horst hoffmann (4.knappe)

188/**28 july 1968**
bayerischer rundfunk recording

tristan und isolde
bayreuth festival orchestra
and chorus
conductor karl böhm
chorus-master wilhelm pitz

unpublished radio broadcast

birgit nilsson (isolde)
grace hoffman (brangäne)
wolfgang windgassen (tristan)
gerd feldhoff (kurwenal)
martti talvela (marke)
reid bunger (melot)
hermin esser (hirt and junger seemann)
kurt moll (steuermann)

189/**29 july 1968**
bayerischer rundfunk broadcast

das rheingold
bayreuth festival orchestra
conductor lorin maazel

unpublished radio broadcast

theo adam (wotan)
janis martin (fricka)
helga dernesch (freia)
marga höffgen (erda)
gerd nienstedt (donner)
hermin esser (froh)
wolfgang windgassen (loge)
gustav neidlinger (alberich)
gerhard stolze (mime)
karl ridderbusch (fasolt)
josef greindl (fafner)
dorothea siebert (woglinde)
elisabeth schwarzenberg (wellgunde)
sieglinde wagner (flosshilde)

190/**30 july 1968**
bayerischer rundfunk broadcast

die walküre
bayreuth festival orchestra
conductor lorin maazel

unpublished radio broadcast

berit lindholm (brünnhilde)
leonie rysanek (sieglinde)
janis martin (fricka)
james king (siegmund)
theo adam (wotan)
josef greindl (hunding)
elisabeth schwarzenberg (gerhilde)
helga dernesch (ortlinde)
gertraud hopf (waltraute)
sieglinde wagner (schwertleite)
liane synek (helmwige)
inger paustian (siegrune)
marie-luise gilles (grimgerde)
unni rugtvedt (rossweisse)

191/**1 august 1968**
bayerischer rundfunk broadcast

siegfried
bayreuth festival orchestra
conductor lorin maazel

unpublished radio broadcast

berit lindholm (brünnhilde)
erika köth (waldvogel)
marga höffgen (erda)
ticho parly (siegfried)
theo adam (wanderer)
gerhard stolze (mime)
gustav neidlinger (alberich)
josef greindl (fafner)

192/**3 august 1968**
bayerischer rundfunk broadcast

götterdämmerung
bayreuth festival orchestra and chorus
conductor lorin maazel
chorus-master wilhelm pitz

unpublished radio broadcast

gladys kuchta (brünnhilde)
helga dernesch (gutrune)
grace hoffman (waltraute)
wolfgang windgassen (siegfried)
thomas stewart (gunther)
josef greindl (hagen)
gustav neidlinger (alberich)
marga höffgen (1.norn)
janis martin (2.norn)
berit lindholm (3.norn)
dorothea siebert (woglinde)
elisabeth schwarzenberg (wellgunde)
sieglinde wagner (flosshilde)

193/**25 july 1969**
bayerischer rundfunk broadcast

der fliegende holländer
bayreuth festival orchestra and chorus
conductor silvio varviso
chorus-master wilhelm pitz

unpublished radio broadcast

leonie rysanek (senta)
unni rugtvedt (mary)
donald mcintyre (holländer)
martti talvela (daland)
jean cox (erik)
rené kollo (steuermann)

194/**26 july 1969**
bayerischer rundfunk broadcast

parsifal
bayreuth festival orchestra and chorus
conductor horst stein
chorus-master wilhelm pitz

cd: house of opera (usa)

ludmilla dvorakova (kundry)
james king (parsifal)
thomas stewart (amfortas)
franz crass (gurnemanz)
karl ridderbusch (titurel)
gerd nienstedt (klingsor)
unni rugtvedt (stimme von oben)
hannelore bode (1.blumenmädchen)
elisabeth schwarzenberg (2.blumenmädchen and 1.knappe)
helga dernesch (3.blumenmädchen)
dorothea siebert (4.blumenmädchen)
ingrit liljeberg (5.blumenmädchen)
sieglinde wagner (6.blumenmädchen and 2.knappe)
hermin esser (1.gralsritter)
bengt rundgren (2.geralsritter)
dieter slembeck (3.knappe)
thomas lehrberger (4.knappe)

bayerischer rundfunk states that it holds a second tape in its archive dated 6 august 1969 (with gwyneth jones in the role of kundry)

140
195/**27 july 1969**
bayerischer rundfunk broadcast

die meistersinger von nürnberg
bayreuth festival orchestra and chorus
conductor berislav klobucar
chorus-master wilhelm pitz

unpublished radio broadcast

helga dernesch (eva)
janis martin (magdalene)
waldemar kmentt (stolzing)
hermin esser (david)
norman bailey (sachs)
karl ridderbusch (pogner)
gerd nienstedt (kothner)
thomas hemsley (beckmesser)
rené kollo (vogelgesang)
dieter slembeck (nachtigall)
sebastian feiersinger (zorn)
erich klaus (eisslinger)
william johns (moser)
heinz feldhoff (ortel)
fritz linke (schwarz)
hans frantzen (foltz)
bengt rundgren (nachtwächter)

196/**28 july 1969**
bayerischer rundfunk broadcast

tristan und isolde
bayreuth festival orchestra and chorus
conductor karl böhm
chorus-master wilhelm pitz

unpublished radio broadcast

cast as for entry no. 188

196/**29 july 1969**
bayerischer rundfunk broadcast

das rheingold
bayreuth festival orchestra
conductor lorin maazel

unpublished radio broadcast

thomas stewart (wotan)
rest of cast as for entry no. 189

197/**30 july 1969**
bayerischer rundfunk broadcast

die walküre
bayreuth festival orchestra
conductor lorin maazel

unpublished radio broadcast

thomas stewart (wotan)
rest of cast as for entry no. 190

198/**1 august 1969**
bayerischer rundfunk broadcast

siegfried
bayreuth festival orchestra
conductor lorin maazel

unpublished radio broadcast

jess thomas (siegfried)
thomas stewart (wanderer)
rest of cast as for entry no. 191

199/**3 august 1969**
bayerischer rundfunk broadcast

götterdämmerung
bayreuth festival orchestra and chorus
conductor lorin maazel
chorus-master wilhelm pitz

unpublished radio broadcast

jess thomas (siegfried)
rest of cast as for entry no. 192

200/**june-august 1970**
recorded by deutsche grammophon during rehearsals and performances; also bayerischer rundfunk broadcast on 2 august 1970

parsifal
bayreuth festival orchestra and chorus
conductor pierre boulez
chorus-master wilhelm pitz

lp: deutsche grammophon 2713 004/2720 034/2721 004/2740 143/ 419 0331
cd: deutsche grammophon 435 7182
excerpts
lp: deutsche grammophon 2721 078/2721 112/2721 113/2737 025/ 410 8551

gwyneth jones (kundry)
james king (parsifal)
franz crass (gurnemanz)
thomas stewart (amfortas)
karl ridderbusch (titurel)
donald mcintyre (klingsor)
marga höffgen (stimme von oben)
hannelore bode (1.blumenmädchen)
margarita kyriaki (2.blumenmädchen)
inger paustian (3.blumenmädchen)
dorothea siebert (4.blumenmädchen)
wendy fine (5.blumenmädchen)
sieglinde wagner (6.blumenmädchen and 2.knappe)
hermin esser (1.gralsritter)
bengt rundgren (2.gralsritter)
elisabeth schwarzenberg (1.knappe)
dieter slembeck (3.knappe)
heinz zednik (4.knappe)

201/**24 july 1970**
bayerischer rundfunk broadcast

tristan und isolde
bayreuth festival orchesrtra
and chorus
conductor karl böhm
chorus-master wilhelm pitz

cd: private edition vienna
this issue is dated august 1970

birgit nilsson (brünnhilde)
grace hoffman (brangäne)
wolfgang windgassen (tristan)
gustav neidlinger (kurwenal)
martti talvela (marke)
reid bunger (melot)
hermin esser (hirt and junger seemann)
bengt rundgren (steuermann)

202/**25 july 1970**
bayerischer rundfunk broadcast

die meistersinger von nürnberg
bayreuth festival orchestra and chorus
conductor hans wallat
chorus-master wilhelm pitz

unpublished radio broadcast

janis martin (eva)
sylvia anderson (magdalene)
jean cox (stolzing)
hermin esser (david)
norman bailey (sachs)
karl ridderbusch (pogner)
thomas hemsley (beckmesser)
gerd nienstedt (kothner)
horst laubenthal (vogelgesang)
dieter slembeck (nachtigall)
robert locha (zorn)
heinz zednik (eisslinger)
georg paskuda (moser)
heinz feldhoff (ortel)
fritz linke (schwarz)
hans franzen (foltz)
bengt rundgren (nachtwächter)

203/**26 july 1970**
bayerischer rundfunk broadcast

das rheingold
bayreuth festival orchestra
conductor horst stein

unpublished radio broadcast

thomas stewart (wotan)
janis martin (fricka)
margarita kyriaki (freia)
marga höffgen (erda)
gerd nienstedt (donner)
rené kollo (froh)
hermin esser (loge)
georg paskuda (mime)
gustav neidlinger (alberich)
karl ridderbusch (fasolt)
bengt rundgren (fafner)
hannelore bode (woglinde)
inger paustian (wellgunde)
sylvia anderson (flosshilde)

204/**27 july 1970**
bayerischer rundfunk broadcast

die walküre
bayreuth festival orchestra
conductor horst stein

unpublished radio broadcast

berit lindholm (brünnhilde)
gwyneth jones (sieglinde)
anna reynolds (fricka)
helge brilioth (siegmund)
thomas stewart (wotan)
karl ridderbusch (hunding)
elisabeth schwarzenberg (gerhilde)
gildis flossmann (ortlinde)
wendy fine (waltraute)
sylvia anderson (schwertleite)
liane synek (helmwige)
inger paustian (siegrune)
faith puleston (grimgerde)
aili purtonen (rossweisse)

205/**29 july 1970**
bayerischer rundfunk broadcast

siegfried
bayreuth festival orchestra
conductor horst stein

unpublished radio broadcast

berit lindholm (brünnhilde)
marga höffgen (erda)
hannelore bode (waldvogel)
jean cox (siegfried)
thomas stewart (wanderer)
georg paskuda (mime)
gustav neidlinger (alberich)
bengt rundgren (fafner)

206/**31 july 1970**
bayerischer rundfunk broadcast

götterdämmerung
bayreuth festival orchestra and chorus
conductor horst stein
chorus-master wilhelm pitz

unpublished radio broadcast

berit lindholm (brünnhilde)
janis martin (gutrune)
anna reynolds (waltraute and 2.norn)
jean cox (siegfried)
norman bailey (gunther)
karl ridderbusch (hagen)
gustav neidlinger (alberich)
marga höffgen (1.norn)
liane synek (3.norn)
hannelore bode (woglinde)
inger paustian (wellgunde)
sylvia anderson (flosshilde)

207/**1 august 1970**
bayerischer rundfunk broadcast

der fliegende holländer
bayreuth festival orchestra and chorus
conductor silvio varviso
chorus-master wilhelm pitz

unpublished radio broadcast

leonie rysanek (senta)
maria von ilosvay (mary)
donald mcintyre (holländer)
hermin esser (erik)
horst laubenthal (steuermann)
martti talvela (daland)

208/**24 july 1971**
bayerischer rundfunk broadcast

parsifal
bayreuth festival orchestra and chorus
conductor eugen jochum
chorus-master wilhelm pitz

cd: golden melodram GM 10059

janis martin (kundry)
sandor konya (parsifal)
thomas stewart (amfortas)
franz crass (gurnemanz)
karl ridderbusch (titurel)
gerd nienstedt (klingsor)
marga höffgen (stimme von oben)
hannelore bode (1.blumenmädchen)
elizabeth volkman (2.blumenmädchen)
inger paustian (3.blumenmädchen)
dorothea siebert (4.blumenmädchen)
wendy fine (5.blumenmädchen)
sieglinde wagner (6.blumenmädchen and 2.knappe)
heribert steinbach (1.gralsritter)
heinz feldhoff (2.gralsritter)
elisabeth schwarzenberg (1.knappe)
hartmann gniffke (3.knappe)
heinz zednik (4.knappe)

209/**25 july 1971**
bayerischer rundfunk broadcast

lohengrin
bayreuth festival orchestra and chorus
conductor silvio varviso
chorus-master wilhelm pitz

unpublished radio broadcast

hannelore bode (elsa)
ludmilla dvorakova (ortrud)
rené kollo (lohengein)
donald mcintyre (telramund)
franz crass (könig heinrich)
ingvar wixell (heerrufer)
heribert steinbach (1.edler)
heinz zednik (2.edler)
hartmann gniffke (3.edler)
heinz feldhoff (4.edler)

210/**26 july 1971**
bayerischer rundfunk broadcast

das rheingold
bayreuth festival orchestra
conductor horst stein

unpublished radio broadcast

theo adam (wotan)
anna reynolds (fricka)
janis martin (freia)
marga höffgen (erda)
gerd nienstedt (donner)
harald ek (froh)
hermin esser (loge)
gustav neidlinger (alberich)
georg paskuda (mime)
karl ridderbusch (fasolt)
peter meven (fafner)
elizabeth volkman (woglinde)
inger paustian (wellgunde)
sylvia anderson (flosshilde)

211/**27 july 1971**
bayerischer rundfunk broadcast

die walküre
bayreuth festival orchestra
conductor horst stein

unpublished radio broadcast

catarina ligendza (brünnhilde)
gwyneth jones (sieglinde)
anna reynolds (fricka)
helge brilioth (siegmund)
theo adam (wotan)
karl ridderbusch (hagen)
elisabeth schwarzenberg (gerhilde)
ursula rhein (ortlinde)
sylvia anderson (waltraute)
glenys loulis (schwertleite)
wendy fine (helmwige)
inger paustian (siegrune)
faith puleston (grimgerde)
sieglinde wagner (rossweisse)

212/**29 july 1971**
bayerischer rundfunk broadcast

siegfried
bayreuth festival orchestra
conductor horst stein

unpublished radio broadcast
excerpts
cd: opernwelt 2002

catarina ligendza (brünnhilde)
elizabeth volkman (waldvogel)
marga höffgen (erda)
jean cox (siegfried)
theo adam (wanderer)
georg paskuda (mime)
gustav neidlinger (alberich)
peter meven (fafner)

213/**31 july 1971**
bayerischer rundfunk broadcast

götterdämmerung
bayreuth festival orchestra and chorus
conductor horst stein
chorus-master wilhelm pitz

unpublished radio broadcast

catarina ligendza (brünnhilde)
janis martin (gutrune)
anna reynolds (waltraute and 2.norn)
jean cox (siegfried)
franz mazura (gunther)
karl ridderbusch (hagen)
gustav neidlinger (alberich)
marga höffgen (1.norn)
wendy fine (3.norn)
elizabeth volkman (woglinde)
inger paustian (wellgunde)
sylvia anderson (flosshilde)

bayerischer rundfunk states that it holds
a second tape in its archive dated
18 august 1970 (with berit lindhilm
in the role of brünnhilde)

214/**august 1971**
recorded by deutsche grammophon at performances during august

der fliegende holländer
bayreuth festival orchestra and chorus
conductor karl böhm
chorus-master wilhelm pitz

lp: deutsche grammophon 2709 040/2720 052/2740 140/413 2911
cd: deutsche grammophon 437 7102
excerpts
lp: deutsche grammophon 2537 024

gwyneth jones (senta)
sieglinde wagner (mary)
thomas stewart (holländer)
karl ridderbusch (daland)
hermin esser (erik)
harald ek (steuermann)

215/**21 july 1972**
bayerischer rundfunk broadcast

tannhäuser
bayreuth festival orchestra and chorus
conductor erich leinsdorf
chorus-master norbert balatsch

unpublished radio broadcast

gwyneth jones (elisabeth and venus)
hugh beresford (tannhäuser)
bernd weikl (wolfram)
hans sotin (landgraf)
harald ek (walther von der vogelweide)
franz mazura (biterolf)
heibert steinbach (heinrich der schreiber)
heinz feldhoff (reinmar von zweter)

bayerischer rundfunk states that it also holds a tape of the dress rehearsal

216/**22 july 1972**
bayerischer rundfunk broadcast

lohengrin
bayreuth festival orchestra and chorus
conductor silvio varviso
chorus-master norbert balatsch

unpublished radio broadcast

hannelore bode (elsa)
ursula schröder-feinen (ortrud)
rené kollo (lohengrin)
donald mcintyre (telramund)
franz crass (könig heinrich)
gerd nienstedt (heerrufer)
heribert steinbach (1.edler)
heinz zednik (2.edler)
hartmann gniffke (3.edler)
heinz feldhoff (4.edler)

152
217/**23 july 1972**
bayerischer rundfunk broadcast

das rheingold
bayreuth festival orchestra
conductor horst stein

unpublished radio broadcast

thomas stewart (wotan)
anna reynolds (fricka)
hannelore bode (freia)
marga höffgen (erda)
gerd nienstedt (donner)
heribert steinbach (froh)
hermin esser (loge)
gustav neidlinger (alberich)
heinz zednik (mime)
karl ridderbusch (fasolt)
hans sotin (fafner)
yoko kawahara (woglinde)
ursula rhein (wellgunde)
ilse gramatzki (flosshilde)

218/**24 july 1972**
bayerischer rundfunk broadcast

die walküre
bayreuth festival orchestra
conductor horst stein

unpublished radio broadcast

catarina ligendza (brünnhilde)
gwyneth jones (sieglinde)
anna reynolds (fricka and siegrune)
james king (siegmund)
thomas stewart (wotan)
karl ridderbusch (hunding)
elisabeth schwarzenberg (gerhilde)
ursula rhein (ortlinde)
michele vilma (waltraute)
katherine pring (schwertleite)
leslie johnson (helmwige)
ilse gramatzki (grimgerde)
sieglinde wagner (rossweisse)

219/**26 july 1972**
bayerischer rundfunk broadcast

siegfried
bayreuth festival orchestra
conductor horst stein

unpublished radio broadcast

catarina ligendza (brünnhilde)
yoko kawahara (waldvogel)
marga höffgen (erda)
jean cox (siegfried)
thomas stewart (wanderer)
gustav neidlinger (alberich)
heinz zednik (mime)
heinz feldhoff (fafner)

220/**28 july 1972**
bayerischer rundfunk broadcast

götterdämmerung
bayreuth festival orchestra and chorus
conductor horst stein
chorus-master norbert balatsch

unpublished radio broadcast

catarina ligendza (brünnhilde)
janis martin (gutrune)
anna reynolds (waltraute and 2.norn)
jean cox (siegfried)
franz mazura (gunther)
karl ridderbusch (hagen)
marga höffgen (1.norn)
ursula schröder-feinen (3.norn)
yoko kawahara (woglinde)
ursula rhein (wellgunde)
ilse gramatzki (flosshilde)

221/**29 july 1972**
bayerischer rundfunk broadcast

parsifal
bayreuth festival orchestra and chorus
conductor eugen jochum
chorus-master norbert balatsch

unpublished radio broadcast

james king (parsifal)
janis martin (kundry)
franz crass (gurnemanz)
theo adam (amfortas)
karl ridderbusch (titurel)
donald mcintyre (klingsor)
marga höffgen (stimme von oben)
hannelore bode (1.blumenmädchen)
elisabeth schwarzenberg (2.blumenmädchen and 1.knappe)
ilse gramatzki (3.blumenmädchen)
yoko kawahara (4.blumenmädchen)
leslie johnson (5.blumenmädchen)
sieglinde wagner (6.blumenmädchen and 2.knappe)
heribert steinach (1.gralsritter)
heinz feldhoff (2.gralsritter)
hartmann gniffke (3.knappe)
heinz zednik (4.knappe)

222/**25 july 1973**
bayerischer rundfunk broadcast

die meistersinger von nürnberg
bayreuth festival orchestra
and chorus
conductor silvio varviso
chorus-master norbert balatsch

unpublished radio broadcast

hannelore bode (eva)
anna reynolds (magdalene)
rené kollo (stolzing)
frieder stricker (david)
karl ridderbusch (sachs)
hans sotin (pogner)
gerd nienstedt (kothner)
klaus hirte (beckmesser)
heribert steinbach (vogelgesang)
hartmann gniffke (nachtigall)
robert licha (zorn)
wolf appel (eisslinger)
norbert orth (moser)
heinz feldhoff (ortel)
hartmut bauer (schwarz)
joszef dene (foltz)
bernd weikl (nachtwächter)

223/**27 july 1973**
bayerischer rundfunk broadcast

parsifal
bayreuth festival orchestra and chorus
conductor eugen jochum
chorus-master norbert balatsch

unpublished radio broadcast

jean cox (parsifal)
janis martin (kundry)
donald mcintyre (amfortas)
franz mazura (gurnemanz)
hans sotin (titurel)
gerd nienstedt (klingsor)
marga höffgen (stimme von oben)
hannelore bode (1.blumenmädchen)
elisabeth schwarzenberg (2.blumenmädchen
  and 1.knappe)
ilse gramatzki (3.blumenmädchen)
yoko kawahara (4.blumenmädchen)
eva randova (5.blumenmädchen)
sieglinde wagner (6.blumenmädchen and
  2.knappe)
heribert steinbach (1.gralsritter)
heinz feldhoff (2.gralsritter)
hartmann gniffke (3.knappe)
heinz zednik (4.knappe)

224/28 july 1973
bayerischer rundfunk broadcast

das rheingold
bayreuth festival orchestra
conductor horst stein

unpublished radio broadcast

theo adam (wotan)
anna reynolds (fricka)
hannelore bode (freia)
marga höffgen (erda)
gerd nienstedt (donner)
heribert steinbach (froh)
hermin esser (loge)
franz mazura (alberich)
heinz zednik (mime)
karl ridderbusch (fasolt)
hartmut bauer (fafner)
yoko kawahara (woglinde)
ursula rhein (wellgunde)
ilse gramatzki (flosshilde)

225/29 july 1973
bayerischer rundfunk broadcast

die walküre
bayreuth festival orchestra
conductor horst stein

unpublished radio broadcast

berit lindholm (brünnhilde)
gwyneth jones (sieglinde)
anna reynolds (fricka and siegrune)
theo adam (wotan)
gerd brenneis (siegmund)
karl ridderbusch (hunding)
elisabeth schwarzenberg (gerhilde)
ursula rhein (ortlinde)
eva randova (waltraute)
katherine pring (schwertleite)
marita napier (helmwige)
ilse gramatzki (grimgerde)
sieglinde wagner (rossweisse)

226/**31 july 1973**
bayerischer rundfunk broadcast

siegfried
bayreuth festival orchestrra
conductor horst stein

unpublished radio broadcast

ursula schröder-feinen (brünnhilde)
yoko kawahara (waldvogel)
marga höffgen (erda)
jean cox (siegfried)
theo adam (wanderer)
heinz zednik (mime)
gustav neidlinger (alberich)
heinz feldhoff (fafner)

227/**2 august 1973**
bayerischer rundfunk broadcast

götterdämmerung
bayreuth festival orchestra and chorus
conductor horst stein
chorus-master norbert balatsch

unpublished radio broadcast

catarina ligendza (brünnhilde)
eva randova (gutrune)
anna reynolds (waltraute and 2.norn)
jean cox (siegfried)
franz mazura (gunther)
karl ridderbusch (hagen)
gustav neidlinger (alberich)
marga höffgen (1.norn)
marita napier (3.norn)
yoko kawahara (woglinde)
ursula rhein (wellgunde)
ilse gramatzki (flosshilde)

228/**3 august 1973**
bayerischer rundfunk broadcast

tannhäuser
bayreuth festival orchestra and chorus
conductor heinrich hollreiser
chorus-master norbert balatsch

unpublished radio broadcast

gerd brenneis (walther von der vogelweide)
rest of cast as for entry no. 215

229/**25 july 1974**
bayerischer rundfunk recording

tristan und isolde
bayreuth festival orchestra and chorus
conductor carlos kleiber
chorus-master norbert balatsch

cd: golden melodram GM 10036
cd: hypnos HYP 254-256
cd: private edition vienna

catarina ligendza (isolde)
yvonne minton (brangäne)
helge brilioth (tristan)
donald mcintyre (kurwenal)
kurt moll (marke)
heribert steinbach (melot)
heinz zednik (hirt and junger seemann)
heinz feldhoff (steuermann)

bayerischer rundfunk states that due to a tape defect act one had to be recorded again at the performance of 3 august 1974

230/**26 july 1974**
bayerischer rundfunk broadcast

tannhäuser
bayreuth festival orchestra and chorus
conductor heinrich hollreiser
chorus-master norbert balatsch

unpublished radio broadcast

hermin esser (tannhäuser)
gerd brenneis (walther von der vogelweide)
rest of cast as for entry no. 215

231/**27 july 1974**
bayerischer rundfunk broadcast and recording by philips at this and further performances in august 1974

die meistersinger von nürnberg
bayreuth festival orchestra and chorus
conductor silvio varviso
chorus-master norbert balatsch

lp: philips 6747 167/6747 243
cd: philips 434 6112
excerpts
lp: philips 412 0251
lp: philips sequenza 6527 108
cd: philips eloquence 468 1852

hannelore bode (eva)
anna reynolds (magdalene)
jean cox (stolzing)
frieder stricker (david)
karl ridderbusch (sachs)
hans sotin (pogner)
gerd nienstedt (kothner)
klaus hirte (beckmesser)
heribert steinbach (vogelgesang)
jozsef dene (nachtigall)
robert licha (zorn)
wolf appel (eisslinger)
norbert orth (moser)
heinz feldhoff (ortel)
hartmut bauer (schwarz)
nikolaus hillebrand (foltz)
bernd weikl (nachtwächter)

232/**28 july 1974**
bayerischer rundfunk broadcast

das rheingold
bayreuth festival orchestra
conductor horst stein

unpublished radio broadcast

donald mcintyre (wotan)
anna reynolds (fricka)
hannelore bode (freia)
marga höffgen (erda)
heribert steinbach (froh)
hermin esser (loge)
heinz zednik (mime)
gerd nienstedt (donner)
franz mazura (alberich)
karl ridderbusch (fasolt)
kurt moll (fafner)
yoko kawahara (woglinde)
ursula rhein (wellgunde)
ilse köhler (flosshilde)

233/**29 july 1974**
bayerischer rundfunk broadcast

die walküre
bayreuth festival orchestra
conductor horst stein

unpublished radio broadcast

roberta knie (brünnhilde)
marita napier (sieglinde)
anna reynolds (fricka and siegrune)
gerd brenneis (siegmund)
donald mcintyre (wotan)
karl ridderbusch (hunding)
hannelore bode (gerhilde)
ursula rhein (ortlinde)
eva randova (waltraute)
helga angervo (schwertleite)
brenda roberts (helmwige)
ilse köhler (grimgerde)
ingrid mayr (rossweisse)

234 / **31 july 1974**
bayerischer rundfunk broadcast

siegfried
bayreuth festival orchestra
conductor horst stein

unpublished radio broadcast

brenda roberts (brünnhilde)
yoko kawahara (waldvogel)
marga höffgen (erda)
jean cox (siegfried)
heinz zednik (mime)
franz mazura (alberich)
donald mcintyre (wanderer)
heinz feldhoff (fafner)

235 / **2 august 1974**
bayerischer rundfunk broadcast

götterdämmerung
bayreuth festival orchestra and chorus
conductor horst stein
chorus-master norbert balatsch

unpublished radio broadcast

gwyneth jones (brünnhilde)
eva randova (gutrune)
anna reynolds (waltraute and 2.norn)
jean cox (siegfried)
gerd nienstedt (gunther)
karl ridderbusch (hagen)
klaus hirte (alberich)
marga höffgen (1.norn)
marita napier (3.norn)
yoko kawahara (woglinde)
ursula rhein (wellgunde)
ilse köhler (flosshilde)

236/**25 july 1975**
bayerischer rundfunk broadcast

parsifal
bayreuth festival orchestra and chorus
conductor horst stein
chorus-master norbert balatsch

unpublished radio broadcast

eva randova (kundry)
rené kollo (parsifal)
bernd weikl (amfortas)
hans sotin (gurnemanz)
karl ridderbusch (titurel)
franz mazura (klingsor)
ortrun wenkel (stimme von oben)
rachel yakar (1.blumenmädchen)
trudeliese schmidt (2.blumenmädchen and 1.knappe)
hanna schwarz (3.blumenmädchen and 2.knappe)
yoko kawahara (4.blumenmädchen)
irja auroora (5.blumenmädchen)
alicia nafé (6.blumenmädchen)
heribert steinbach (1.gralsritter)
nikolaus hillebrand (2.gralsritter)
martin finke (3.knappe)
martin egel (4.knappe)

237/**26 july 1975**
bayerischer rundfunk broadcast

tristan und isolde
bayreuth festival orchestra and chorus
conductor carlos kleiber
chorus-master norbert balatsch

cd: exclusive EX92 T 54-56
jonathan brown (tristan und isolde on record) dates the performance as 4 august 1975

nikolaus hillebrand (steuermann)
rest of cast as for entry no. 229

bayerischer rundfunk states that it holds a second tape in its archive dated 4 august 1975

238/**27 july 1975**
bayerischer rundfunk broadcast

die meistersinger von nürnberg
bayreuth festival orchestra and chorus
conductor heinrich hollreiser
chorus-master norbert balatsch

unpublished radio broadcast

marita napier (eva)
martin egel (nachtigall)
martin finke (moser)
rest of cast as for entry no. 231

239/**28 july 1975**
bayerischer rundfunk broadcast

das rheingold
bayreuth festival orchestra
conductor horst stein

unpublished radio broadcast

donald mcintyre (wotan)
anna reynolds (fricka)
rachel yakar (freia)
marga höffgen (erda)
gerd nienstedt (donner)
heribert steinbach (froh)
hermin esser (loge)
gustav neidlinger (alberich)
heinz zednik (mime)
karl ridderbusch (fasolt)
kurt moll (fafner)
yoko kawahara (woglinde)
trudeliese schmidt (wellgunde)
hanna schwarz (flosshilde)

240/**29 july 1975**
bayerischer rundfunk broadcast

die walküre
bayreuth festival orchestra
conductor horst stein

unpublished radio broadcast

gwyneth jones (brünnhilde)
marita napier (sieglinde)
anna reynolds (fricka and siegrune)
donald mcintyre (wotan)
james king (siegmund)
karl ridderbusch (hunding)
rachel yakar (gerhilde)
irja auroora (ortlinde)
eva randova (waltraute)
ortrun wenkel (schwertleite)
jeanne hieronymi (helmwige)
trudeliese schmidt (grimgerde)
hanna schwarz (rossweisse)

241/**31 july 1975**
bayerischer rundfunk broadcast

siegfried
bayreuth festival orchestra
conductor horst stein

unpublished radio broadcast

gwyneth jones (brünnhilde)
yoko kawahara (waldvogel)
marga höffgen (erda)
jean cox (siegfried)
donald mcintyre (wanderer)
heinz zednik (mime)
gustav neidlinger (alberich)
nikolaus hillebrand (fafner)

242/**2 august 1975**
bayerischer rundfunk broadcast

götterdämmerung
bayreuth festival orchestra and chorus
conductor horst stein
chorus-master norbert balatsch

unpublished radio broadcast

gwyneth jones (brünnhilde)
eva randova (gutrune)
anna reynolds (waltraute and 2.norn)
jean cox (siegfried)
franz mazura (gunther)
karl ridderbusch (hagen)
gustav neidlinger (alberich)
marga höffgen (1.norn)
marita napier (3.norn)
yoko kawahara (woglinde)
trudliese schmidt (wellgunde)
hanna schwarz (flosshilde)

243/**23 july 1976**
bayerischer rundfunk broadcast of bayreuth festival centenary celebration

die meistersinger von nürnberg: overture and closing scene (festwiese)
bayreuth festival orchestra and chorus
conductor karl böhm
chorus-master norbert balatsch

unpublished radio broadcast

hannelore bode (eva)
ilse gramatzki (magdalene)
rené kollo (stolzing)
frieder stricker (david)
theo adam (sachs)
hans sotin (pogner)
gerd nienstedt (kothner)
klaus hirte (beckmesser)
heribert steinbach (vogelgesang)
martin egel (nachtigall)
robert licha (zorn)
wolf appel (eisslinger)
heinz zednik (moser)
heinz feldhoff (ortel)
hartmut bauer (schwarz)
kurt rydl (foltz)

244/**24 july 1976**
bayerischer rundfunk broadcast

das rheingold
bayreuth festival orchestra
conductor pierre boulez

unpublished radio broadcast

donald mcintyre (wotan)
eva randova (fricka)
rachel yakar (freia)
ortrun wenkel (erda)
jerker arvidson (donner)
heribert steinbach (froh)
heinz zednik (loge)
wolf appel (mime)
zoltan kelemen (alberich)
matti salminen (fasolt)
bengt rundgren (fafner)
yoko kawahara (woglinde)
ilse gramatzki (wellgunde)
adelheid krauss (flosshilde)

245/**25 july 1976**
bayerischer rundfunk broadcast

die walküre
bayreuth festival orchestra
conductor pierre boulez

unpublished radio broadcast

gwyneth jones (brünnhilde)
hannelore bode (sieglinde)
eva randova (fricka)
peter hofmann (siegmund)
donald mcintyre (wotan)
matti salmimen (hunding)
rachel yakar (gerhilde)
irja auroora (ortlinde)
doris soffel (waltraute)
adelheid krauss (schwertleite)
katie clarke (helmwige)
alicia nafé (siegrune)
ilse gramatzki (grimgerde)
elisabeth glauser (rossweisse)

246/**27 july 1976**
bayerischer rundfunk broadcast

siegfried
bayreuth festival orchestra
conductor pierre boulez

unpublished radio broadcast

gwyneth jones (brünnhilde)
yoko kawahara (waldvogel)
hanna schwarz (erda)
rené kollo (siegfried)
heinz zednik (mime)
donald mcintyre (wanderer)
zoltan kelemen (alberich)
bengt rundgren (fafner)

247/**29 july 1976**
bayerischer rundfunk broadcast

götterdämmerung
bayreuth festival orchestra and chorus
conductor pierre boulez
chorus-master norbert balatsch

unpublished radio broadcast

gwyneth jones (brünnhilde)
irja auroora (gutrune)
yvonne minton (waltraute)
jess thomas (siegfried)
jerker arvidson (gunther)
karl ridderbusch (hagen)
zoltan kelemen (alberich)
ortrun wenkel (1.norn)
dagmar trabert (2.norn)
hannelore bode (3.norn)
yoko kawahara (woglinde)
ilse gramatzki (wellgunde)
adelheid krauss (flosshilde)

248/**30 july 1976**
bayerischer rundfunk broadcast

tristan und isolde
bayreuth festival orchestra
and chorus
conductor carlos kleiber
chorus-master norbert balatsch

lp: legendary recordings LR 196
jonathan brown (tristan und isolde on record) incorrectly dates the performance as 29 july 1976

catarina ligendza (isolde)
yvonne minton (brangäne)
spas wenkoff (tristan)
donald mcintyre (kurwenal)
karl ridderbusch (marke)
heribert steinbach (melot)
heinz zednik (hirt and junger seemann)
heinz feldhoff (steuermann)

249/**31 july 1976**
bayerischer rundfunk broadcast

parsifal
bayreuth festival orchestra
and chorus
conductor horst stein
chorus-master norbert balatsch

unpublished radio broadcast

peter hofmann (parsifal)
eva randova (kundry)
bernd weikl (amfortas)
hans sotin (gurnemanz)
karl ridderbusch (titurel)
franz mazura (klingsor)
ortrun wenkel (stimme von oben)
rachel yakar (1.blumenmädchen)
carol richardson (2.blumenmädchen
* and 1.knappe)*
adelheid krauss (3.blumenmädchen
* and 2.knappe)*
yoko kawahara (4.blumenmädchen)
irja auroora (5.blumenmädchen)
alicia nafé (6.blumenmädchen)
heribert steinbach (1.gralsritter)
heinz feldhoff (2.gralsritter)
heinz zednik (3.knappe)
martin egel (4.knappe)

250/**23 july 1977**
bayerischer rundfunk broadcast

tannhäuser
bayreuth festival orchestra
and chorus
conductor colin davis
chorus-master norbert balatsch

unpublished radio broadcast

gwyneth jones (elisabeth and venus)
hermin esser (tannhäuser)
bernd weikl (wolfram)
hans sotin (landgraf)
robert schunk (walther v.d.vogelweide)
franz mazura (biterolf)
john pickering (heinrich der schreiber)
heinz feldhoff (reinmar von zweter)

251/**25 july 1977**
bayerischer rundfunk broadcast

parsifal
bayreuth festival orchestra
and chorus
conductor horst stein
chorus-master norbert balatsch

unpublished radio broadcast

rené kollo (parsifal)
hanna schwarz (stimme von oben, 3.
* blumenmädchen and 2.knappe)*
norma sharp (1.blumenmädchen)
carmen reppel (4.blumenmädchen)
inga nielsen (5.blumenmädchen)
ilse gramatzki (6.blumenmädchen
* and 1.knappe)*
robert schunk (1.gralsritter)
rest of cast as for entry no. 249

252/**26 july 1977**
bayerischer rundfunk broadcast

das rheingold
bayreuth festival orchestra
conductor pierre boulez

unpublished radio broadcast

donald mcintyre (wotan)
eva randova (fricka)
carmen reppel (freia)
hanna schwarz (erda)
martin egel (donner)
siegfried jerusalem (froh)
heinz zednik (loge)
wolf appel (mime)
zoltan kelemen (alberich)
heikki roivanen (fasolt)
matti salminen (fafner)
norma sharp (woglinde)
ilse gramatzki (wellgunde)
cornelia wulkopf (flosshilde)

253/**27 july 1977**
bayerischer rundfunk broadcast

die walküre
bayreuth festival orchestra
conductor pierre boulez

unpublished radio broadcast

gwyneth jones (brünnhilde)
hannelore bode (sieglinde)
eva randova (fricka)
robert schunk (siegmund)
donald mcintyre (wotan)
matti salminen (hunding)
carmen reppel (gerhilde)
astrid schirmer (ortlinde)
gabriele schnaut (waltraute)
patricia payne (schwertleite)
katie clarke (helmwige)
cornelia wulkopf (siegrune)
ilse gramatzki (grimgerde)
elisabeth glauser (rossweisse)

254/**29 july 1977**
bayerischer rundfunk broadcast

siegfried
bayreuth festival orchestra
connductor pierre boulez

unpublished radio broadcast

gwyneth jones (brünnhilde)
norma sharp (waldvogel)
hanna schwarz (erda)
rené kollo (siegfried)
donald mcintyre (wanderer)
heinz zednik (mime)
zoltan kelemen (alberich)
matti salminen (fafner)

255/**31 july 1977**
bayerischer rundfunk broadcast

götterdämmerung
bayreuth festival orchestra and chorus
conductor pierre boulez
chorus-master norbert balatsch

unpublished radio broadcast

gwyneth jones (brünnhilde)
hannelore bode (gutrune)
yvonne minton (waltraute)
manfred jung (siegfried)
franz mazura (gunther)
karl ridderbusch (hagen)
zoltan kelemen (alberich)
patricia payne (1.norn)
gabriele schnaut (2.norn)
katie clarke (3.norn)
norma sharp (woglinde)
ilse gramatzki (wellgunde)
cornelia wulkopf (flosshilde)

256/**25 july 1978**
bayerischer rundfunk broadcast

der fliegende holländer
bayreuth festival orchestra
and chorus
conductor dennis russell davies
chorus-master norbert balatsch

unpublished radio broadcast

lisbeth balslev (senta)
anny schlemm (mary)
simon estes (holländer)
matti salminen (daland)
robert schunk (erik)
francisco araiza (steuermann)

257/**26 july 1978**
bayerischer rundfunk broadcast

parsifal
bayreuth festival orchestra
and chorus
conductor horst stein
chorus-master norbert balatsch

unpublished radio broadcast

dunja vezcovic (kundry)
peter hofmann (parsifal)
bernd weikl (amfortas)
theo adam (gurnemanz)
matti salminen (titurel)
franz mazura (klingsor)
hanna schwarz (stimme von oben, 2.knappe
 and 3.blumenmädchen)
norma sharp (1.blumenmädchen)
carol richardson (2.blumenmädchen)
carmen reppel (4.blumenmädchen)
kumiko oshita (5.blumenmädchen)
ilse gramatzki (6.blumenmädchen and
 1.knappe)
john pickering (1.gralsritter)
heinz feldhoff (2.gralsritter)
helmut pampuch (3.knappe)
martin egel (4.knappe)

258/**27 july 1978**
bayerischer rundfunk broadcast

tannhäuser
bayreuth festival orchestra and chorus
conductor colin davis
chorus-master norbert balatsch

unpublished radio broadcast

eva marton (elisabeth and venus)
spas wenkoff (tannhäuser)
rest of cast as for entry no. 250

259/**28 july 1978**
bayerischer rundfunk broadcast

das rheingold
bayreuth festival orchestra
conductor pierre boulez

unpublished radio broadcast

donald mcintyre (wotan)
hanna schwarz (fricka)
carmen reppel (freia)
ortrun wenkel (erda)
martin egel (donner)
siegfried jerusalem (froh)
heinz zednik (loge)
helmut pampuch (mime)
zoltan kelemen (alberich)
heikki toivanen (fasolt)
matti salminen (fafner)
norma sharp (woglinde)
ilse gramatzki (wellgunde)
marga schiml (flosshilde)

260/**29 july 1978**
bayerischer rundfunk broadcast

die walküre
bayreuth festival orchestra
conductor pierre boulez

unpublished radio broadcast

gwyneth jones (brünnhilde)
hannelore bode (sieglinde)
hanna schwarz (fricka)
peter hofmann (siegmund)
donald mcintyre (wotan)
matti salminen (hunding)
carmen reppel (gerhilde)
maria de francesca-cavazza (ortlinde)
gabriele schnaut (waltraute)
gwendolyn killebrew (schwerleite)
katie clarke (helmwige)
marga schiml (siegrune)
ilse gramatzki (grimgerde)
elisabeth glauser (rossweisse)

261/**31 july 1978**
bayerischer rundfunk broadcast

siegfried
bayreuth festival orchestra
conductor pierre boulez

unpublished radio broadcast

gwyneth jones (brünnhilde)
norma sharp (waldvogel)
ortrun wenkel (erda)
rené kollo (siegfried)
donald mcintyre (wanderer)
heinz zednik (mime)
zoltan kelemen (alberich)
matti salminen (fafner)

262/**2 august 1978**
bayerischer rundfunk broadcast

götterdämmerung
bayreuth festival orchestra and chorus
conductor pierre boulez
chorus-master norbert balatsch

unpublished radio broadcast

gwyneth jones (brünnhilde)
hannelore bode (gutrune)
gwendolyn killebrew (waltraute)
manfred jung (siegtfried)
franz mazura (gunther)
fritz hübner (hagen)
zoltan kelemen (alberich)
ortrun wenkel (1.norn)
gabriele schnaut (2.norn)
katie clarke (3.norn)
norma sharp (woglinde)
ilse gramatzki (wellgunde)
marga schiml (flosshilde)

263/ **august-september 1978**
unitel film sessions without audience: first complete wagner performance filmed in bayreuth festspielhaus

tannhäuser
bayreuth festival orchestra and chorus
conductor colin davis
chorus-master norbert balatsch

vhs video: philips 070 4123/070 5123
laserdisc: philips 070 4121/070 5121
excerpts
vhs video: philips 070 1583

gwyneth jones (elisabeth and venus)
spas wenkoff (tannhäuser)
bernd weikl (wolfram)
hans sotin (landgraf)
robert schunk (walther von der vogelweide)
john pickering (heinrich der schreiber)
franz mazura (biterolf)
heinz feldhoff (reinmar von zweter)
klaus brettschneider (ein junger hirt)

roles of elisabeth and venus sung in stage performances at the 1978 bayreuth festival by eva marton

264/**25 july 1979**
bayerischer rundfunk broadcast

lohengrin
bayreuth festival orchestra and chorus
conductor edo de waart
chorus-master norbert balatsch

unpublished radio broadcast

karan armstrong (elsa)
ruth hesse (ortrud)
peter hofmann (lohengrin)
leif roar (telramund)
hans sotin (könig heinrich)
bernd weikl (heerrufer)
toni krämer (1.edler)
helmut pampuch (2.edler)
martin egel (3.edler)
karl schreiber (4.edler)

265/**26 july 1979**
bayerischer rundfunk broadcast

der fliegende holländer
bayreuth festival orchestra
and chorus
conductor dennis russell davies
chorus-master norbert balatsch

unpublished radio broadcast

hermin esser (erik)
rest of cast as for entry no. 256

266/**27 july 1979**
bayerischer rundfunk broadcast

parsifal
bayreuth festival orchestra
and chorus
conductor horst stein
chorus-master norbert balatsch

unpublished radio broadcast

siegfried jerusalem (parsifal)
marga schiml (5.blumenmädcen)
rest of cast as for entry no. 257

267/**28 july 1979**
bayerischer rundfunk broadcast

das rheingold
bayreuth festival orchestra
conductor pierre boulez

unpublished radio broadcast

donald mcintyre (wotan)
hanna schwarz (fricka)
carmen reppel (freia)
ortrun wenkel (erda)
martin egel (donner)
siegfried jerusalem (froh)
heinz zednik (loge)
helmut pampuch (mime)
hermann becht (alberich)
matti salminen (fasolt)
fritz hübner (fafner)
norma sharp (woglinde)
ilse gramatzki (wellgunde)
marga schiml (flosshilde)

268/**29 july 1979**
bayerischer rundfunk broadcast

die walküre
bayreuth festival orchestra
conductor pierre boulez

unpublished radio broadcast

gwyneth jones (brünnhilde)
jeannine altmeyer (sieglinde)
hanna schwarz (fricka)
donald mcintyre (wotan)
peter hofmann (siegmund)
matti salminen (hunding)
carmen reppel (gerhilde)
karen middleton (ortlinde)
gabriele schnaut (waltraute)
gwendolyn killebrew (schwertleite)
katie clarke (helmwige)
marga schiml (siegrune)
ilse gramatzki (grimergde)
elisabeth glauser (rossweisse)

269/**31 july 1979**
bayerischer rundfunk broadcast

siegfried
bayreuth festival orchestra
conductor pierre boulez

unpublished radio broadcast

gwyneth jones (brünnhilde)
norma sharp (waldvogel)
ortrun wenkel (erda)
manfred jung (siegfried)
hans sotin (wanderer)
heinz zednik (mime)
hermann becht (alberich)
fritz hübner (fafner)

270/**2 august 1979**
bayerischer rundfunk broadcast

götterdämmerung
bayreuth festival orchestra and chorus
conductor pierre boulez
chorus-master norbert balatsch

unpublished radio broadcast

gwyneth jones (brünnhilde)
jeannine altmeyer (gutrune)
gwendolyn killebrew (waltraute)
manfred jung (siegfried)
franz mazura (gunther)
fritz hübner (hagen)
hermann becht (alberich)
ortrun wenkel (1.norn)
gabriele schnaut (2.norn)
katie clarke (3.norn)
norma sharp (woglinde)
ilse gramatzki (wellgunde)
marga schiml (flosshilde)

271/**august-september 1979**
unitel film and bayerischer rundfunk sound sessions without audience

die walküre
bayreuth festival orchestra
conductor pierre boulez

lp: philips 6769 071/6769 074
cd: philips 434 4222/434 4202
vhs video: philips 070 4023/070 4073/070 4303
laserdisc: philips 070 4021/070 4301/070 5021
dvd video: philips 070 4029/070 4079
excerpts
cd: philips 426 2112/446 5102/446 6142
vhs video: philips 070 1583/070 1773
complete editions on vhs video and laserdisc also included film documentary on the making of the bayreuth centenary ring

cast as for entry no. 268

272/**august-september 1979**
unitel film and bayerischer rundfunk sound sessions without audience

siegfried
bayreuth festival orchestra
conductor pierre boulez

lp: philips 6769 072/6769 074
cd: philips 434 4232/434 4202
vhs video: philips 070 4033/070 4073/070 4303
laserdisc: philips 070 4031/070 4301/070 5031
dvd video: philips 070 4039/070 4079
excerpts
cd: philips 426 2112/446 6152
vhs video: philips 070 1583/070 1773

donald mcintyre (wanderer)
rest of cast as for entry no. 269

273/**25 july 1980**
bayerischer rundfunk broadcast

parsifal
bayreuth festival orchestra
and chorus
conductor horst stein
chorus-master norbert balatsch

unpublished radio broadcast

dunja vejzovic (kundry)
siegfried jerusalem (parsifal)
bernd weikl (amfortas)
theo adam (gurnemanz)
matti salminen (titurel)
franz mazura (klingsor)
hanna schwarz (stimme von oben,
 3.blumenmädchen and 2.knappe)
norma sharp (1.blumenmädchen)
carol richardson (2.blumenmädchen)
carmen reppel (4.blumenmädchen)
marga schiml (5.blumenmädchen)
ilse gramatzki (6.blumenmädchen and
 1.knappe)
volker horn (1.gralsritter)
dieter brencke (2.gralsritter)
helmut pampuch (3.knappe)
martin egel (4.knappe)

274/**26 july 1980**
bayerischer rundfunk broadcast

der fliegende holländer
bayreuth festival orchestra
and chorus
conductor dennis russell davies
chorus-master norbert balatsch

unpublished radio broadcast

david kuebler (steuermann)
rest of cast as for entry no. 256

275/**27 july 1980**
bayerischer rundfunk broadcast

lohengrin
bayreuth festival orchestra
and chorus
conductor woldemar nelsson
chorus-master norbert balatsch

unpublished radio broadcast

cast as for entry no. 264

276/**28 july 1980**
bayerischer rundfunk broadcast

das rheingold
bayreuth festival orchestra
conductor pierre boulez

unpublished radio broadcast

donald mcintyre (wotan)
hanna schwarz (fricka)
carmen reppel (freia)
ortrun wenkel (erda)
martin egel (donner)
siegfried jerusalem (froh)
heinz zednik (loge)
helmut pampuch (mime)
hermann becht (alberich)
matti salmimen (fasolt)
fritz hübner (fasolt)
norma sharp (woglinde)
ilse gramatzki (wellgunde)
marga schiml (flosshilde)

277/**29 july 1980**
bayerischer rundfunk broadcast

die walküre
bayreuth festival orchestra
conductor pierre boulez

unpublished radio broadcast

gwyneth jones (brünnhilde)
jeannine altmeyer (sieglinde)
hanna schwarz (fricka)
donald mcintyre (wotan)
peter hofmann (siegmund)
matti salminen (hunding)
carmen reppel (gerhilde)
karen middleton (ortlinde)
gabriele schnaut (waltraute)
katie clarke (helmwige)
gwendolyn killebrew (schwertleite)
marga schiml (siegrune)
ilse gramatzki (grimgerde)
elisabeth glauser (rossweisse)

278/**31 july 1980**
bayerischer rundfunk broadcast

siegfried
bayreuth festival orchestrra
conductor pierre boulez

unpublished radio broadcast

gwyneth jones (brünnhilde)
norma sharp (waldvogel)
ortrun wenkel (erda)
manfred jung (siegfried)
donald mcintyre (wanderer)
heinz zednik (mime)
hermann becht (alberich)
fritz hübner (fafner)

279/**2 august 1980**
bayerischer rundfunk broadcast

götterdämmerung
bayreuth festival orchestra and chorus
conductor pierre boulez
chorus-master norbert balatsch

unpublished radio broadcast

gwyneth jones (brünnhilde)
jeannine altmeyer (gutrune)
gwendolyn killebrew (waltraute)
manfred jung (siegfried)
franz mazura (gunther)
fritz hübner (hagen)
ortrun wenkel (1.norn)
gabriele schnaut (2.norn)
katie clarke (3.norn)
norma sharp (woglinde)
ilse gramatzki (wellgunde)
marga schiml (flosshilde)

280/**august-september 1980**
unitel film and bayerischer rundfunk sound sessions without audience

das rheingold
bayreuth festival orchestra
conductor pierre boulez

lp: philips 6769 070/6769 074
cd: philips 434 4212/434 4202
vhs video: philips 070 4013/070 4073/070 4303
laserdisc: philips 070 4011/070 4301/070 5011
dvd video: philips 070 4019/070 4079
excerpts
cd: philips 426 2112/446 6132
vhs video: philips 070 1583/070 1773

cast as for entry no. 276

281/**august-september 1980**
unitel film and bayerischer rundfunk sound sessions without audience

götterdämmerung
bayreuth festival orchestra and chorus
conductor pierre boulez
chorus-master norbert balatsch

lp: philips 6769 073/6769 074
cd: philips 434 4242/434 4202
vhs video: philips 070 4043/070 4073/070 4303
laserdisc: philips 070 4041/070 4301/070 5041
dvd video: philips 070 4049/070 4079
excerpts
cd: philips 426 2112/446 6132
vhs video: philips 070 1585/070 1773

cast as for entry no. 279

282/**25 july 1981**
bayerischer rundfunk broadcast

tristan und isolde
bayreuth festival orchestra and chorus
conductor daniel barenboim
chorus-master norbert balatsch

unpublished radio broadcast

johanna meier (isolde)
hanna schwarz (brangäne)
rené kollo (tristan)
hermann becht (kurwenal)
matti salminen (marke)
robert schunk (melot and junger seemann)
helmut pampuch (hirt)
martin egel (steuermann)

283/**26 july 1981**
bayerischer rundfunk broadcast

die meistersinger von nürnberg
bayreuth festival orchestra and chorus
conductor mark elder
chorus-master norbert balatsch

unpublished radio broadcast

mari anne häggander (eva)
marga schiml (magdalene)
siegfried jerusalem (stolzing)
graham clark (david)
bernd weikl (sachs)
manfred schenk (pogner)
jef vermeersch (kothner)
hermann prey (beckmesser)
david kuebler (vogelgesang)
martin egel (nachtigall)
udo holdorf (zorn)
toni krämer (eisslinger)
helmut pampuch (moser)
sandor solyom-nagy (ortel)
heinz klaus ecker (schwarz)
dieter schweikart (foltz)
matthias hölle (nachtwächter)

284/**27 july 1981**
bayerischer rundfunk broadcast

der fliegende holländer
bayreuth festival orchestra
and chorus
conductor peter schneider
chorus-master norbert balatsch

unpublished radio broadcast

cast as for entry no. 274

285/**28 july 1981**
bayerischer rundfunk broadcast

lohengrin
bayreuth festival orchestra
and chorus
conductor woldemar nelsson
chorus-master norbert balatsch

unpublished radio broadcast

cast as for entry no. 264

286/**29 july 1981**
bayerischer rundfunk broadcast

parsifal
bayreuth festival orchestra
and chorus
conductor horst stein
chorus-master norbert balatsch

unpublished radio broadcast

manfred jung (parsifal)
eva randova (kundry)
donald mcintyre (amfortas)
hans sotin (gurnemanz)
matti salminen (titurel)
leif roar (klingsor)
hanna schwaez (stimme von oben, 2.knappe
 and 3.blumenmädchen)
norma sharp (1.blumenmädchen)
carol richardson (2.blumenmäschen)
mari anne häggander (4.blumenmädchen)
marga schiml (5.blumenmädchen and
 1.knappe)
margit neubauer (6.blumenmädchen)
toni krämer (1.gralsroiter)
heinz klaus ecker (2.gralsritter)
helmut pampuch (3.knappe)
martin egel (4.knappe)

287/**august 1981**
unitel film sessions without audience

parsifal
bayreuth festival orchestra and chorus
conductor horst stein
chorus-master norbert balatsch

vhs video: philips 070 4103/070 5103
laserdisc: philips 070 4101/070 5101/CDV 507-519
excerpts
vhs video: philips 070 1583

siegfried jerusalem (parsifal)
rest of cast as for entry no. 286

288/**25 july 1982**
bayerischer rundfunk broadcast

parsifal
bayreuth festival orchestra and chorus
conductor james levine
chorus-master norbert balatsch

cd: private edition vienna
this edition incorrectly dated 24 july 1982

leonie rysanek (kundry)
peter hofmann (parsifal)
simon estes (amfortas)
hans sotin (gurnemanz)
matti salminen (titurel)
franz mazura (klingsor)
hanna schwarz (stimme von oben and 3.blumenmädchen)
monika schmitt (1.blumenmädchen)
anita soldh (2.blumenmädchen)
laurent gérimont (4.blumenmädchen)
deborah sasson (5.blumenmädchen)
margit neubauer (6.blumenmädchen)
toni krämer (1.gralsritter)
matthias hölle (2.gralsritter)
ruthild engert-ely (1.knappe)
sabine fues (2.knape)
helmut pampuch (3.knappe)
peter maus (4.knappe)

289/**26 july 1982**
bayerischer rundfunk broadcast

tristan und isolde
bayreuth festival orchestra and chorus
conductor daniel barenboim
chorus-master norbert balatsch

unpublished radio broadcast

cast as for entry no. 282

290/**27 july 1982**
bayerischer rundfunk broadcast

der fliegende holländer
bayreuth festival orchestra and chorus
conductor peter schneider
chorus-master norbert balatsch

unpublished radio broadcast

cast as for entry no. 274

291/**28 july 1982**
bayerischer rundfunk broadcast

die meistersinger von nürnberg
bayreuth festival orchestra and chorus
conductor horst stein
chorus-master norbert balatsch

unpublished radio broadcast

cast as for entry no. 283

292/**29 july 1982**
bayerischer rundfunk broadcast

lohengrin
bayreuth festival orchestra and chorus
conductor woldemar nelsson
chorus-master norbert balatsch

unpublished radio broadcast

karan armstrong (elsa)
elizabeth connell (ortrud)
peter hofmann (lohengrin)
leif roar (telramund)
siegfried vogel (könig heinrich)
berns weikl (heerrufer)
toni krämer (1.edler)
helmut pampuch (2.edler)
martin egel (3.edler)
heinz klaus ecker (4.edler)

293/**august 1982**
unitel film and cbs sound sessions without audience

lohengrin
bayreuth festival orchestra and chorus
conductor woldemar nelsson
chorus-master norbert balatsch

lp: cbs 79503
cd: sony M3K 79503/M3K 38594
vhs video: philips 070 4113/070 5113
laserdisc: philips 070 4111/070 5111
excerpts
vhs video: philips 070 1583

cast as for entry no. 292

294/**13 february 1983**
bayerischer rundfunk broadcast of commemoration to mark centenary of wagner's death

liszt: von der wiege bis zum grab, symphonic poem
wagner: siegfried idyll

bayreuth festival orchestra
conductor pierre boulez

unpublished radio broadcast

295/**24 july 1983**
bayerischer rundfunk broadcast

die meistersinger von nürnberg
bayreuth festival orchestra and chorus
conductor horst stein
chorus-master norbert balatsch

unpublished radio broadcast

mari anne häggander (eva)
marga schiml (magdalene)
siegfried jerusalem (stolzing)
graham clark (david)
bernd weikl (sachs)
manfred schenk (pogner)
hermann prey (beckmesser)
jef vermeersch (kothner)
andras molnar (vogelgesang)
martin egel (nachtigall)
udo holdorf (zorn)
toni krämer (eisslinger)
helmut pampuch (moser)
sandor solyom-nagy (ortel)
heinz klaus ecker (schwarz)
dieter schweikart (foltz)
matthias hölle (nachtwächter)

296/**25 july 1983**
bayerischer rundfunk broadcast

das rheingold
bayreuth festival orchestra
conductor georg solti

unpublished radio broadcast

doris soffel (fricka)
anita soldh (freia)
anne gjevang (erda)
siegmund nimsgern (wotan)
heinz-jürgen demitz (donner)
maldwyn davies (froh)
manfred jung (loge)
peter haage (mime)
hermann becht (alberich)
manfred schenk (fasolt)
dieter schweikart (fafner)
agnes habereder (woglinde)
diana montague (wellgunde)
birgitta svenden (flosshilde)

297/**26 july 1983**
bayerischer rundfunk broadcast

die walküre
bayreuth festival orchestra
conductor georg solti

unpublished radio broadcast

hildegard behrens (brünnhilde)
jeannine altmeyer (sieglinde)
doris soffel (fricka)
siegfried jerusalem (siegmund)
siegmund nimsgern (wotan)
matthias hölle (hunding)
anita soldh (gerhilde)
anne evans (ortlinde)
ingrid karrasch (waltraute)
anne wilkens (schwertleite)
agnes habereder (helmwige)
diana montague (siegrune)
ruthild engert-ely (grimgerde)
anne gjevang (rossweisse)

298/**28 july 1983**
bayerischer rundfunk broadcast

siegfried
bayreuth festival orchesrea
conductor georg solti

unpublished radio broadcast

hildegard behrens (brünnhilde)
sylvia greenberg (waldvogel)
anne gjevang (erda)
manfred jung (siegfried)
siegmund nimsgern (wanderer)
peter haage (mime)
hermann becht (alberich)
dieter schweikart (fafner)

299/**30 july 1983**
bayerischer rundfunk broadcast

götterdämmerung
bayreuth festival orchestra and chorus
conductor georg solti
chorus-master norbert balatsch

unpublished radio broadcast

hildegard behrens (brünnhilde)
josephine barstow (gutrune)
brigitte fassbaender (waltraute)
manfred jung (siegfried)
bent norup (gunther)
aage haugland (hagen)
hermann becht (alberich)
anne gjevang (1.norn)
anne wilkens (2.norn)
anne evans (3.norn)
agnes habereder (woglinde)
diana montague (wellgunde)
birgitta svenden (flosshilde)

300/31 july 1983
bayerischer rundfunk broadcast

tristan und isolde
bayreuth festival orchestra
and chorus
conductor daniel barenboim
chorus-master norbert balatsch

unpublished radio broadcast

johanna meier (isolde)
hanna schwarz (brangäne)
spas wenkoff (tristan)
hermann becht (kurwenal)
graham clark (melot and seemann)
helmut pampuch (hirt)
martin egel (steuermann)

301/1 august 1983
bayerischer rundfunk broadcast

parsifal
bayreuth festival orchestra
and chorus
conductor james levine
chorus-master norbert balatsch

unpublished radio broadcast

cast as for entry no. 288

302/september-october 1983
unitel film sessions without audience

tristan und isolde
bayreuth festival orchestra
and chorus
conductor daniel barenboim
chorus-master norbert balatsch

vhs video: philips 070 4093/070 5093
laserdisc: philips 070 4091/070 5091
excerpts
vhs video: philips 070 1583

rené kollo (tristan)
robert schunk (melot and seemann)
rest of cast as for entry no. 300

303/**25 july 1984**
bayerischer rundfunk broadcast

der fliegende holländer
bayreuth festival orchestra
and chorus
conductor woldemar nelsson
chorus-master norbert balatsch

unpublished radio broadcast

lisbeth balslev (senta)
anny schlemm (mary)
simon estes (holländer)
matti salminen (daland)
robert schunk (erik)
graham clark (steuermann)

304/**26 july 1984**
bayerischer rundfunk broadcast

parsifal
bayreuth festival orchestra
and chorus
conductor james levine
conductor norbert balatsch

unpublished radio broadcast

peter hofmann (parsifal)
waltraud meier (kundry)
simon estes (amfortas)
hans sotin (gurnemanz)
franz mazura (klingsor)
matti salminen (titurel)
ruthild engert-ely (stimme von oben and
 1.knappe)
monika schmitt (1.blumenmädchen)
anita soldh (2.blumenmädchen)
elfie hobarth (3.blumenmädchen)
christine obermayr (4.blumenmädchen)
deborah sasson (5.blumenmädchen)
margit neubauer (6.blumenmädchen)
michael pabst (1.gralsritter)
matthias hölle (2.gralsritter)
sabine fues (2.knappe)
helmut pampuch (3.knappe)
peter maus (4.knappe)

305/**27 july 1984**
bayerischer rundfunk broadcast

das rheingold
bayreuth festival orchestra
conductor peter schneider
peter schneider replaced georg
solti as conductor

unpublished radio broadcast

siegmund nimsgern (wotan)
hanna schwarz (fricka)
anita soldh (freia)
anne gjevang (erda)
johann-werner prein (donner)
timothy jenkins (froh)
norbert orth (loge)
peter haage (mime)
hermann becht (alberich)
manfred schenk (fasolt)
aage haugland (fafner)
agnes habereder (woglinde)
jane turner (wellgunde)
birgitta svenden (flosshilde)

306/**28 july 1984**
bayerischer rundfunk broadcast

die walküre
bayreuth festival orchestra
conductor peter schneider
peter schneider replaced georg
solti as conductor

unpublished radio broadcast

hildegard behrens (brünnhilde)
jeannine altmeyer (sieglinde)
hanna schwarz (fricka)
siegfried jerusalem (siegmund)
siegmund nimsgern (wotan)
matthias hölle (hunding)
anita soldh (gerhilde)
sophia larson (ortlinde)
ingrid karrasch (waltraute)
anne wilkens (schwertleite)
agnes habereder (helmwige)
jane turner (siegrune)
birgitta svenden (grimgerde)
anne gjevang (rossweisse)

307/**30 july 1984**
bayerischer rundfunk broadcast

siegfried
bayreuth festival orchestra
conductor peter schneider
peter schneider replaced georg solti as conductor

unpublished radio broadcast

hildegard behrens (brünnhilde)
hildegard heichele (waldvogel)
anne gjevang (erda)
manfred jung (siegfried)
siegmund nimsgern (wanderer)
peter haage (mime)
hermann becht (alberich)
aage haugland (fafner)

308/**1 august 1984**
bayerischer rundfunk broadcast

götterdämmerung
bayreuth festival orchestra and chorus
conductor peter schneider
chorus-master norbert balatsch
peter schneider replaced georg solti as conductor

unpublished radio broadcast

hildegard behrens (brünnhilde)
sophia larson (gutrune)
brigitte fassbaender (waltraute)
manfred jung (siegfried)
franz mazura (gunther)
aage haugland (hagen)
hermann becht (alberich)
anne gjevang (1.norn)
anne wilkens (2.norn)
anne evans (3.norn)
agnes habereder (woglinde)
jane turner (wellgunde)
birgitta svenden (flosshilde)

309/**2 august 1984**
bayerischer rundfunk broadcast

die meistersinger von nürnberg
bayreuth festival orchestra and chorus
conductor horst stein
chorus-master norbert balatsch

unpublished radio broadcast

mari-anne häggander (eva)
marga schiml (magdalene)
siegfried jerusalem (stolzing)
graham clark (david)
bernd weikl (sachs)
manfred schenk (pogner)
jef vermeersch (kothner)
hermann prey (beckmesser)
andras molnar (vogelgesang)
martin egel (nachtigall)
udo holdorf (zorn)
peter maus (eisslinger)
helmut pampuch (moser)
sandor solyom-nagy (ortel)
heinz klaus ecker (schwarz)
dieter schweikart (foltz)
matthias hölle (nachtwächter

*310/***august 1984**
unitel film sessions without audience

die meistersinger von nürnberg
bayreuth festival orchestra and chorus
conductor horst stein
chorus-master norbert balatsch

vhs video: philips 070 4133/070 5133
laserdisc: philips 070 4131/070 5131
dvd video: deutsche grammophon 073 4160

cast as for entry no. 309

*311/*25 july 1985
bayerischer rundfunk broadcast

tannhäuser
bayreuth festival orchestra and chorus
conductor giuseppe sinopoli
chorus-master norbert balatsch

unpublished radio broadcast

cheryl studer (elisabeth)
gabriele schnaut (venus)
richard versalle (tannhäuser)
wolfgang brendel (wolfram)
robert schunk (walther von der vogelweide)
siegfried vogel (biterolf)
andras molnar (heinrich der schreiber)
sandor solyom-nagy (reinmar von zweter)
brigitte lindner (ein junger hirt)

*312/*26 july 1985
bayerischer rundfunk broadcast

parsifal
bayreuth festival orchestra and chorus
conductor james levine
chorus-master norbert balatsch

unpublished radio broadcast

susan roberts (2.blumenmädchen)
alison browner (4.blumenmädchen)
rest of cast as for entry no. 304

313/27 july 1985
bayerischer rundfunk broadcast

das rheingold
bayreuth festival orchestra
conductor peter schneider

unpublished radio broadcast

siegmund nimsgern (wotan)
hanna schwarz (fricka)
lucy peacock (freia)
anne gjevang (erda)
johann-werner prien (donner)
timothy jenkins (froh)
manfred jung (loge)
peter haage (mime)
hermann becht (alberich)
hans tschammer (fasolt)
dieter schweikart (fafner)
agnes habereder (woglinde)
silvia herman (wellgunde)
birgitta svenden (flosshilde)

314/28 july 1985
bayerischer rundfunk broadcast

die walküre
bayreuth festival orchestra
conductor peter schneider

unpublished radio broadcast

hildegard behrens (brünnhilde)
jeannine altmeyer (sieglinde)
hanna schwarz (fricka)
siegfried jerusalem (siegmund)
siegmund nimsgern (wotan)
matthias hölle (hunding)
lucy peacock (gerhilde)
sophia larson (ortlinde)
ingrid karrasch (waltraute)
ruthild engert-ely (schwertleite)
agnes habereder (helmwige)
margit neubauer (siegrune)
birgitta svenden (grimgerde)
isolde elchlepp (rossweisse)

315/**30 july 1985**
bayerischer rundfunk broadcast

siegfried
bayreuth festival orchestra
conductor peter schneider

unpublished radio broadcast

hildegaqrd behrens (brünnhilde)
hilde leidland (waldvogel)
anne gjevang (erda)
toni krämer (siegfried)
siegmund nimsgern (wanderer)
peter haage (mime)
hermann becht (alberich)
dieter schweikart (fafner)

316/**1 august 1985**
bayerischer rundfunk broadcast

götterdämmerung
bayreuth festival orchestra and chorus
conductor peter schneider
chorus-master norbert balatsch

unpublished radio broadcast

hildegard behrens (brünnhilde)
sophia larson (gutrune)
hanna schwarz (waltraute and 2.norn)
manfred jung (siegfried)
franz mazura (gunther)
fritz hübner (hagen)
hermann becht (alberich)
anne gjevang (1.norn)
gabriele schnaut (3.norn)
agnes habereder (woglinde)
silvia herman (wellgunde)
birgitta svenden (flosshilde)

317/**2 august 1985**
bayerischer rundfunk broadcast

der fliegende holländer
bayreuth festival orchestra and chorus
conductor woldemar nelsson
chorus-master norbert balatsch

unpublished radio broadcast

cast as for entry no. 303

318/**august 1985**
sound recording by philips during performances

parsifal
bayreuth festival orchestra and chorus
conductor james levine
chorus-master norbert balatsch

lp: philips 416 8421
cd: philips 416 8422/434 6162/464 7562
excerpts
cd: philips 446 5102/446 6222

cast as for entry no. 312

319/**august-september 1985**
unitel film sessions without audience

der fliegende holländer
bayreuth festival orchestra and chorus
conductor woldemar nelsson
chorus-master norbert balatsch

lp: philips 416 3001
cd: philips 416 3002/434 5992
vhs video: philips 070 4070 4063/070 5063
laserdisc: philips 070 4061/070 5061
dvd video: deutsche grammophon 070 4041

cast as for entry no. 303

320/**25 july 1986**
bayerischer rundfunk broadcast

tristan und isolde
bayreuth festival orchestra and chorus
conductor daniel barenboim
chorus-master norbert balatsch

unpublished radio broadcast

jeannine altmeyer (isolde)
waltraud meier (brangäne)
peter hofmann (tristan)
ekkehard wlaschiha (kurwenal)
matti salminen (marke)
robert schunk (melot)
helmut pampuch (hirt)
martin egel (steuermann)
graham clark (junger seemann)

321/**26 july 1986**
bayerischer rundfunk broadcast

tannhäuser
bayreuth festival orchestra and chorus
conductor giuseppe sinopoli
chorus-master norbert balatsch

unpublished radio broadcast

cheryl studer (elisabeth)
gabriele schnaut (venus)
richard versalle (tannhäuser)
wolfgang brendel (wolfram)
hans sotin (landgraf)
robert schunk (walther von der vogelweide)
siegfried vogel (biterolf)
kurt schreibmayer (heinrich der schreiber)
sandor solyom-nagy (reinmar von zweter)
brigitte lindner (ein junger hirt)

322/**27 july 1986**
bayerischer rundfunk broadcast

das rheingold
bayreuth festival orchestra
conductor peter schneider

unpublished radio broadcast

cast as for entry no. 313

323/**28 july 1986**
bayerischer rundfunk broadcast

die walküre
bayreuth festival orchestra
conductor peter schneider

unpublished radio broadcast

gabriele schnaut (sieglinde)
rest of cast as for entry no. 314

324/**30 july 1986**
bayerischer rundfunk broadcast

siegfried
bayreuth festival orchestra
conductor peter schneider

unpublished radio broadcast

cast as for entry no. 315

325/**31 july 1986**
bayerischer rundfunk broadcast and bayerisches fernsehen direct transmission

concert to commemorate centenary of the death of franz liszt:
piano concerto no 2; a faust symphony
bayreuth festival orchestra and chorus
conductor daniel barenboim
chorus-master norbert balatsch

unpublished radio broadcast and video recording

robert schunk
krystian zimerman

326/**1 august 1986**
bayerischer rundfunk broadcast

götterdämmerung
bayreuth festival orchestra and chorus
conductor peter schneider
chorus-master norbert balatsch

unpublished radio broadcast

aage haugland (hagen)
rest of cast as for entry no. 316

327/**2 august 1986**
bayerischer rundfunk broadcast

die meistersinger von nürnberg
bayreuth festival orchestra and chorus
conductor horst stein
chorus-master norbert balatsch

unpublished radio broadcast

cast as for entry no. 309

328/**25 july 1987**
bayerischer rundfunk broadcast

lohengrin
bayreuth festival orchestra and chorus
conductor peter schneider
chorus-master norbert balatsch

unpublished radio broadcast

nadine secunde (elisabeth)
gabriele schnaut (ortrud)
paul frey (lohengrin)
ekkehard wlaschiha (telramund)
manfred schenk (könig heinrich)
james johnson (heerrufer)
clemens bieber (1.edler)
helmut pampuch (2.edler)
robert riener (3.edler)
heinz klaus ecker (4.edler)

329/**26 july 1987**
bayerischer rundfunk broadcast

parsifal
bayreuth festival orchestra and chorus
conductor daniel barenboim
chorus-master norbert balatsch

unpublished radio broadcast

cast as for entry no. 312

330/**27 july 1987**
bayerischer rundfunk broadcast

tristan und isolde
bayreuth festival orchestra and chorus
conductor daniel barenboim
chorus-master norbert balatsch

unpublished radio broadcast

catarina ligendza (isolde)
hanna schwarz (brangäne)
peter hofmann (tristan)
bodo brinkmann (kurwenal)
matti salminen (marke)
graham clark (melot and junger seemann)
martin egel (steuermann)

331/**28 july 1987**
bayerischer rundfunk broadcast

tannhäuser
bayreuth festival orchestra and chorus
conductor giuseppe sinopoli
chorus-master norbert balatsch

unpublished radio broadcast

cheryl studer (elisabeth)
sophia larson (venus)
richard versalle (tannhäuser)
wolfgang brendel (wolfram)
hans sotin (landgraf)
kurt schreibmayer (walther von der vogelweide)
siegfried vogel (biterolf)
clemens bieber (heinrich der schreiber)
sandor solyom-nagy (reinmar von zweter)
brigitte lindner (ein junger hirt)

332/**29 july 1987**
bayerischer rundfunk broadcast

die meistersinger von nürnberg
bayreuth festival orchestra and chorus
conductor michael schonwandt
chorus-master norbert balatsch

unpublished radio broadcast

lucy peacock (eva)
marga schiml (magdalene)
reiner goldberg (stolzing)
graham clark (david)
bernd weikl (sachs)
manfred schenk (pogner)
jef vermeersch (kothner)
alan opie (beckmesser)
kurt schreibmayer (vogelgesang)
martin egel (nachtigall)
udo holdorf (zorn)
peter maus (eisslinger)
sandor solyom-nagy (ortel)
heinz klaus ecker (schwarz)
dieter schweikart (foltz)
matthias hölle (nachtwächter)

333/**26 july 1988**
bayerischer rundfunk broadcast

parsifal
bayreuth festival orchestra and chorus
conductor james levine
chorus-master norbert balatsch

unpublished radio broadcast

siegfried jerusalem (parsifal)
waltraud meier (kundry)
donald mcintyre (amfortas)
hans sotin (gurnemanz)
matthias hölle (titurel)
franz mazura (klingsor)
hitomi katagiri (stimme von oben)
deborah sasson (1.blumenmädchen)
hellen kwon (2.blumenmädchen)
hilde leidland (3.blumenmädchen)
marie-claire o'reirdan (4.blumenmädchen)
marianne rorholm (5.blumenmädchen and 1.knappe)
jane turner (6.blumenmädchen)
kurt schreibmayer (1.gralsritter)
dieter schweikart (2.gralsritter)
annette küttenbaum (2.knappe)
helmut pampuch (3.knappe)
peter maus (4.knappe)

334/**27 july 1988**
bayerischer rundfunk broadcast

das rheingold
bayreuth festival orchestra
conductor daniel barenboim

unpublished radio broadcast

john tomlinson (wotan)
linda finnie (fricka)
eva johansson (freia)
anne gjevang (erda)
bodo brinkmann (donner)
kurt schreibmayer (froh)
graham clark (loge)
helmut pampuch (mime)
günter von kannen (alberich)
matthias hölle (fasolt)
philip kang (fafner)
hilde leidland (woglinde)
annette küttenbaum (wellgunde)
jane turner (flosshilde)

335/**28 july 1988**
bayerischer rundfunk broadcast

die walküre
bayreuth festival orchestra
conductor daniel barenboim

unpublished radio broadcast

deborah polaski (brünnhilde)
nadine secunde (sieglinde)
linda finnie (fricka and siegrune)
peter hofmann (siegmund)
john tomlinson (wotan)
matthias hölle (hunding)
eva johansson (gerhilde)
lia frey-rabine (ortlinde)
silvia herman (waltraute)
hitomi hatagiri (schwertleite)
eva maria bundschuh (helmwige)
uta priew (grimgerde)
hebe dijkstra (rossweisse)

336/**30 july 1988**
bayerischer rundfunk broadcast

siegfried
bayreuth festival orchestrra
conductor daniel barenboim

unpublished radio broadcast

deborah polaski (brünnhilde)
hilde leidland (waldvogel)
anne gjevang (erda)
sirgfried jerusalem (siegfried)
franz mazura (wanderer)
graham clark (mime)
günter von kannen (alberich)
philip kang (fafner)

337/**1 august 1988**
bayerischer rundfunk broadcast

götterdämmerung
bayreuth festival orchestra and chorus
conductor daniel barenboim
chorus-master norbert balatsch

unpublished radio broadcast

deborah polaski (brünnhilde)
eva maria bundschuh (gutrune)
waltraud meier (waltraute)
reiner goldberg (siegfried)
bodo brinkmann (gunther)
philip kang (hagen)
günter von kannen (alberich)
anne gjevang (1.norn)
linda finnie (2.norn)
lia frey-rabine (3.norn)
hilde leidland (woglinde)
annette küttenbaum (wellgunde)
jane turner (flosshilde)

338/**25 july 1989**
bayerischer rundfunk broadcast

parsifal
bayreuth festival orchestra and chorus
conductor james levine
chorus-master norbert balatsch

unpublished radio broadcast

william pell (parsifal)
waltraud meier (kundry)
bernd weikl (amfortas)
hans sotin (gurnemanz)
siegfried vogel (titurel)
franz mazura (klingsor)
hitomi katagiri (stimme von oben)
deborah sasson (1.blumenmädchen)
christiane hossfeld (2.blumenmädchen)
hilde leidland (3.blumenmädchen)
rebecca littig (4.blumenmädchen)
alexandra bergmeister (5.blumenmädchen)
jane turner (6.blumenmädchen)
richard brunner (1.gralsritter)
sandor solyom-nagy (2.gralsritter)
carmen anhorn (1.knappe)
annette küttenbaum (2.knappe)
helmut pampuch (3.knappe)
peter maus (4.knappe)

339/**26 july 1989**
bayerischer rundfunk broadcast

lohengrin
bayreuth festival orchestra and chorus
conductor peter schneider
chorus-master norbert balatsch

unpublished radio broadcast

cheryl studer (elsa)
gabriele schnaut (ortrud)
paul frey (lohengrin)
ekkehard wlaschiha (telramund)
manfred schenk (könig heinrich)
eike wilm schulte (heerrufer)
clemens bieber (1.edler)
helmut pampuch (2.edler)
robert riener (3.edler)
heinz klaus ecker (4.edler)

340/**27 july 1989**
bayerischer rundfunk broadcast

das rheingold
bayreuth festival orchestra
conductor daniel barenboim

unpublished radio broadcast

siegfried vogel (fasolt)
rest of cast as for entry no. 334

341/**28 july 1989**
bayerischer rundfunk broadcast

die walküre
bayreuth festival orchestra
conductor daniel barenboim

unpublished radio broadcast

anne evans (brünnhilde)
philip kang (hunding)
ruth gross-floeren (ortlinde)
rest of cast as for entry no. 335

342/**30 july 1989**
bayerischer rundfunk broadcast

siegfried
bayreuth festival orchestra
conductor daniel barenboim

unpublished radio broadcast

anne evans (brünnhilde)
john tomlinson (wanderer)
rest of cast as for entry no. 336

343/**1 august 1989**
bayerischer rundfunk broadcast

götterdämmerung
bayreuth festival orchestra and chorus
conductor daniel barenboim
chorus-master norbert balatsch

unpublished radio broadcast

anne evans (brünnhilde)
siegfried jerusalem (siegfried)
uta priew (3.norn)
rest of cast as for entry no. 337

344/**2 august 1989**
bayerischer rundfunk broadcast

tannhäuser
bayreuth festival orchestra and chorus
conductor giuseppe sinopoli
chorus-master norbert balatsch

unpublished radio broadcast

cheryl studer (elisabeth)
ruthild engert-ely (venus)
richard versalle (tannhäuser)
wolfgang brendel (wolfram)
hans sotin (landgraf)
william pell (walther von der vogelweide)
siegfried vogel (biterolf)
clemens bieber (heinrich der schreiber)
sandor solyom-nagy (reinmar von zweter)
joy robinson (ein junger hirt)

345/**august 1989**
unitel film sessions without audience

tannhäuser
bayreuth festival orchestra and chorus
conductor giuseppe sinopoli
chorus-master norbert balatsch

laserdisc: polygram (japan) 070 5351

cast as for entry no. 344

346 / **3 september 1989 / tokyo bunkamara theatre**
japanese radio recording of guest performance by bayreuth festival

tannhäuser
bayreuth festival orchestra and chorus
conductor giuseppe sinopoli
chorus-master norbert balatsch

unpublished radio broadcast

cast as for entry no. 344

347 / **5 september 1989 / tokyo bunkamara theatre**
japanese radio recording of guest performance by bayreuth festival

lohengrin act one prelude; die meistersinger von nürnberg act one prelude; lohengrin act two
concert performance
bayreuth festival orchestra and chorus
conductor giuseppe sinopoli
chorus-master norbert balatsch

unpublished radio broadcast

reiner goldberg (lohengrin)
elizabeth connell (elsa)
uta priew (ortrud)
ekkehard wlaschiha (telramund)
manfred schenk (könig heinrich)
eike wilm schulte (heerrufer and 3.edler)
clemens bieber (1.edler)
william pell (2.edler)
sandor solyom-nagy (4.edler)

348 / **8 september 1989 / tokyo bunkamara theatre**
japanese radio recording of guest performance by bayreuth festival

siegfried idyll; der fliegende holländer overture; parsifal act three
concert performance
bayreuth festival orchestra and chorus
conductor giuseppe sinopoli
chorus-master norbert balatsch

unpublished radio broadcast

reiner goldberg (parsifal)
manfred schenk (gurnemanz)
ekkehard wlaschiha (amfortas)

349/july 1990
unitel film sessions without audience

lohengrin
bayreuth festival orchestra
and chorus
conductor peter schneider
chorus-master norbert balatsch

cd: philips 434 6022
excerpts
cd: philips 446 5102
video recording remains unpublished

paul frey (lohengrin)
cheryl studer (elsa)
gabriele schnaut (ortrud)
ekkehard wlaschiha (telramund)
manfred schenk (könig heinrich)
eike wilm schulte (heerrufer)
clemens bieber (1.edler)
helmut pampuch (2.edler)
robert riener (3.edler)
heinz klaus ecker (4.edler)

350/25 july 1990
bayerischer rundfunk broadcast

der fliegende holländer
bayreuth festival orchestra and chorus
conductor giuseppe sinopoli
chorus-master norbert balatsch

unpublished radio broadcast

elizabeth connell (senta)
barbara bornemann (mary)
bernd weikl (holländer)
hans sotin (daland)
reiner goldberg (erik)
clemens bieber (steuermann)

351/26 july 1990
bayerischer rundfunk broadcast

lohengrin
bayreuth festival orchestra
and chorus
conductor peter schneider
chorus-master norbert balatsch

unpublished radio broadcast

cast as for entry no. 349

352/**27 july 1990**
bayerischer rundfunk broadcast

das rheingold
bayreuth festival orchestra
conductor daniel barenboim

unpublished radio broadcast

cast as for entry no. 334

353/**28 july 1990**
bayerischer rundfunk broadcast

die walküre
bayreuth festival orchestra
conductor daniel barenboim

unpublished radio broadcast

anne evans (brünnhilde)
nadine secunde (sieglinde)
linda finnie (fricka)
john tomlinson (wotan)
poul elming (siegmund)
matthias hölle (hunding)
eva johansson (gerhilde)
ruth gross-floeren (ortlinde)
uta priew (waltraute)
hitomi katagiri (schwertleite)
eva maria bundschuh (helmwigr)
christina hagen (grimgerde)
hebe dijkstra (rossweisse)

354/**30 july 1990**
bayerischer rundfunk broadcast

siegfried
bayreuth festival orchestra
conductor daniel barenboim

unpublished radio broadcast

cast as for entry no. 342

355/**1 august 1990**
bayerischer rundfunk broadcast

götterdämmerung
bayreuth festival orchestra
and chorus
conductor daniel barenboim
chorus-master norbert balatsch

unpublished radio broadcast

cast as for entry no. 343

356/**2 august 1990**
bayerischer rundfunk broadcast

parsifal
bayreuth festival orchestra and chorus
conductor james levine
chorus-master norbert balatsch

unpublished radio broadcast

william pell (parsifal)
waltraud meier (kundry)
bernd weikl (amfortas)
hans sotin (gurnemanz)
matthias hölle (titurel)
günter von kannen (klingsor)
hitimi karagiri (stimme von oben)
carmen anhorn (blumenmädchen and 1.knappe)
alexandra bergmeister (blumenmädchen)
christiane hossfeld (blumenmädchen)
rebecca littig (blumenmädchen)
marie-claire o'riordan (blumenmädchen)
jane turner (blumenmädchen)
richard brunner (1.gralsritter)
sandor solyom-nagy (2.gralsritter)
annette küttenbaum (2.knappe)
helmut pampuch (3.knappe)
peter maus (4.knappe)

357/june-july 1991
*unitel film sessions and sound
recording without audience*

das rheingold
bayreuth festival orchestra
conductor daniel barenboim

cd: teldec 4509 911222/
  2564 620912
vhs video: teldec 4509 911223
dvd video: teldec 2564 623182
*2564 620912 includes a dvd video
sampler of excerpts*

*john tomlinson (wotan)
linda finnie (fricka)
eva johannson (freia)
birgitta svenden (erda)
kurt schreibmayer (froh)
graham clark (loge)
helmut pampuch (mime)
bodo brinkmann (donner)
günter von kannen (alberich)
matthias hölle (fasolt)
philip kang (fafner)
hilde leidland (woglinde)
annette küttenbaum (wellgunde)
jane turner (flosshilde)*

358/june-july 1991
*unitel film sessions and sound
recording without audience*

götterdämmerung
bayreuth festival orchestra
and chorus
conductor daniel barenboim
chorus-master norbert balatsch

cd: teldec 4509 941942/
  2564 620912
vhs video: teldec 4509 041943
dvd video: teldec 2564 623212
*2564 620912 includes a dvd video
sampler of excerpts*

*anne evans (brünnhilde)
eva maria bundschuh (gutrune)
waltraud meier (waltraute)
siegfried jerusalem (siegfried)
bodo brinkmann (gunther)
philip kang (hagen)
günter von kannen (alberich)
birgitta svenden (1.norn)
linda finnie (2.norn)
uta priew (3.norn)
hilde leidland (woglinde)
annette küttenbaum (wellgunde)
jane turner (flosshilde)*

359/**26 july 1991**
bayerischer rundfunk broadcast

parsifal
bayreuth festival orchestra and chorus
conductor james levine
chorus-master norbert balatsch

unpublished radio broadcast

franz mazura (klingsor)
rest of cast as for entry no. 356

360/**27 july 1991**
bayerischer rundfunk broadcast

das rheingold
bayreuth festival orchestra
conductor daniel barenboim

unpublished radio broadcast

cast as for entry no. 357

361/**28 july 1991**
bayerischer rundfunk broadcast

die walküre
bayreuth festival orchestra
conductor daniel barenboim

unpublished radio broadcast

deborah polaski (brünnhilde)
rest of cast as for entry no. 353

362/**30 july 1991**
bayerischer rundfunk broadcast

siegfried
bayreuth festival orchestra
conductor daniel barenboim

unpublished radio broadcast

cast as for entry no. 342

363/**1 august 1991**
bayerischer rundfunk broadcast

götterdämmerung
bayreuth festival orchestra
and chorus
conductor daniel barenboim
chorus-master norbert balatsch

unpublished radio broadcast

manfred schenk (hagen)
rest of cast as for entry no. 358

364/**2 august 1991**
bayerischer rundfunk broadcast

der fliegende holländer
bayreuth festival orchestra and chorus
conductor giuseppe sinopoli
chorus-master norbert balatsch

unpublished radio broadcast

sabine hass (senta)
hebe dijkstra (mary)
bernd weikl (holländer)
hans sotin (daland)
reiner goldberg (erik)
clemens bieber (steuermann)

365/**june-july 1992**
*unitel film sessions and sound
recording without sudience*

die walküre
bayreuth festival orchestra
conductor daniel barenboim

cd: teldec 4509 911862/
    2564 620912
vhs video: teldec 4509 911233
dvd video: teldec 2564 623192
*2564 620912 includes a dvd video
sampler of excerpts*

*anne evans (brünnhilde)
nadine secunde (sieglinde)
linda finnie (fricka and siegrune)
john tomlinson (wotan)
poul elming (siegmund)
matthias hölle (hunding)
eva johansson (gerhilde)
ruth gross-floeren (ortlinde)
shirley close (waltraute)
hitomi karagiri (schwerleite)
eva maria bundschuh (helmwige)
birgitta svenden (grimgerde)
hebe dijkstra (rossweisse)*

366/**june-july 1992**
*unitel film sessions and sound
recording without sudience*

siegfried
bayreuth festival orchestra
conductor daniel barenboim

cd: teldec 4509 941932/
    2564 620912
vhs video: teldec 4509 941933
dvd video: teldec 2564 623202
*2564 620912 includes a dvd video
sampler of excerpts*

*anne evans (brünnhilde)
hilde leidland (waldvogel)
birgitta svenden (erda)
siegfried jerusalem (siegfried)
john tomlinson (wanderer)
graham clark (mime)
günter von kannen (alberich)
philip kang (fafner)*

367/**25 july 1992**
bayerischer rundfunk broadcast

tannhäuser
bayreuth festival orchestra
and chorus
conductor donald runnicles
chorus-master norbert balatsch

unpublished radio broadcast

tina kieberg (elisabeth)
uta priew (venus)
wolfgang schmidt (tannhäuser)
eike wilm schulte (wolfram)
manfred schenk (landgraf)
richard brunner (walther von der vogelweide)
ekkehard wlaschiha (biterolf)
clemens bieber (heinrich der schreiber)
sandor solyom-nagy (reinmar von zweter)
christiane hossfeld (ein junger hirt)

368/**26 july 1992**
bayerischer rundfunk broadcast

das rheingold
bayreuth festival orchestra
conductor daniel barenboim

unpublished radio broadcast

cast as for entry no. 357

369/**27 july 1992**
bayerischer rundfunk broadcast

die walküre
bayreuth festival orchestra
conductor daniel barenboim

unpublished radio broadcast

deborah polaski (brünnhilde)
rest of cast as for entry no. 365

370/**29 july 1992**
bayerischer rundfunk broadcast

siegfried
bayreuth festival orchestra
conductor daniel barenboim

unpublished radio broadcast

cast as for entry no. 366

371/**31 july 1992**
bayerischer rundfunk broadcast

götterdämmerung
bayreuth festival orchestra
and chorus
conductor daniel barenboim
chorus-master norbert balatsch

cast as for entry no. 358

372/**1 august 1992**
bayerischer rundfunk broadcast

der fliegende holländer
bayreuth festival orchestra
and chorus
conductor giuseppe sinopoli
chorus-master norbert balatsch

unpublished radio broadcast

cast as for entry no. 364

373/**2 august 1992**
bayerischer rundfunk broadcast

parsifal
bayreuth festival orchestra
and chorus
conductor james levine
chorus-master norbert balatsch

unpublished radio broadcast

poul elming (parsifal)
waltraud meier (kundry)
bernd weikl (amfortas)
manfred schenk (gurnemanz)
matthias hölle (titurel)
franz mazura (klingsor)
hitomi katagiri (stimme von oben)
alexandra bergmeister (blumenmädchen)
christiane hossfeld (blumenmädchen)
rebecca littig (blumenmädchen)
marie claire o'riordan (blumenmädchen)
jane turner (blumenmädchen)
alina wodnika (blumenmädchen and 1.knappe)
richard brunner (1.gralstitter)
sandor solyom-nagy (2.gralsritter)
annette küttenbaum (2.knappe)
helmut pampuch (3.knappe)
peter maus (4.knappe)

374/**17 august 1992**
bayerischer rundfunk broadcast

parsifal
bayreuth festival orchestra
and chorus
conductor james levine
chorus-master norbert balatsch

unpublished radio broadcast

placido domingo (parsifal)
rest of cast as for entry no. 373

375/**25 july 1993**
bayerischer rundfunk broadcast

tristan und isolde
bayreuth festival orchestra and chorus
conductor daniel barenboim
chorus-master norbert balatsch

cd: house of opera (usa)

waltraud meier (isolde)
uta priew (brangäne)
siegfried jerusalem (tristan)
falk struckmann (kurwenal)
john tomlinson (marke)
poul elming (melot and junger seemann)
peter maus (hirt)
sandor solyom-nagy (steuermann)

376/**26 july 1993**
bayerischer rundfunk broadcast

tannhäuser
bayreuth festival orchestra and chorus
conductor donald runnicles
chorus-master norbert balatsch

unpublished radio broadcast

cast as for entry no. 367

377/**27 july 1993**
bayerischer rundfunk broadcast

der fliegende holländer
bayreuth festival orchestra and chorus
conductor giuseppe sinopoli
chorus-master norbert balatsch

unpublished radio broadcast

cast as for entry no. 364

378/**28 july 1993**
bayerischer rundfunk broadcast

lohengrin
bayreuth festival orchestra
and chorus
conductor peter schneider
chorus-master norbert balatsch

unpublished radio broadcast

paul frey (lohengrin)
eva johannson (else)
isolde eschlepp (ortrud)
ekkehard wlaschiha (telramund)
hans sotin (landgraf)

379/**29 july 1993**
bayerischer rundfunk broadcast

parsifal
bayreuth festival orchestra and chorus
conductor james levine
chorus-master norbert balatsch

unpublished radio broadcast

placido domingo (parsifal)
deborah polaski (kundry)
bernd weikl (amfortas)
hans sotin (gurnemanz)
matthias hölle (titurel)
franz mazura (klingsor)
mette ejsing (stimme von oben)
joyce guyer (1.blumenmädchen)
rebecca littig (2.blumenmädchen)
christiane hossfeld (3.blumenmädchen)
alexandra bergmeister (4.blumenmädchen)
jane turner (5.blumenmädchen and 2.knappe)
marie-claire o'reirdan (6.blumenmädchen)
richard brunner (1.gralsritter)
sandor solyom-nagy (2.gralsritter)
sarah fryer (1.knappe)
helmut pampuch (3.knappe)
peter maus (4.knappe)

380/**25 july 1994**
bayerischer rundfunk broadcast

parsifal
bayreuth festival orchestra
and chorus
conductor giuseppe sinopoli
chorus-master norbert balatsch

unpublished radio broadcast

poul elming (parsifal)
uta priew (kundry)
rest of cast as for entry no. 379

381/**26 july 1994**
bayerischer rundfunk broadcast

das rheingold
bayreuth festival orchestra
conductor james levine

unpublished radio broadcast

john tomlinson (wotan)
hanna schwarz (fricka)
nina stemme (freia)
birgitta svenden (erda)
falk struckmann (donner)
richard brunner (froh)
siegfried jerusalem (loge)
manfred jung (mime)
rené pape (fasolt)
eric halfvarson (fafner)
ekkehard wlaschiha (alberich)
joyce guyer (woglinde)
sarah fryer (wellgunde)
jane turner (flosshilde)

382/**27 july 1994**
bayerischer rundfunk broadcast

die walküre
bayreuth festival orchestra
conductor james levine

unpublished radio broadcast

deborah polaski (brünnhilde)
tina kieberg (sieglinde)
hanna schwarz (fricka)
poul elming (siegmund)
john tomlinson (wotan)
hans sotin (hunding)
anna linden (gerhilde)
mary lloyd-davies (ortlinde)
violeta urmana (waltraute)
mette ejsing (schwertleite)
frances ginzer (helmwige)
dalia schaechter (siegrune)
birgitta svenden (grimgerde)
hebe dijkstra (rossweisse)

383/**29 july 1994**
bayerischer rundfunk broadcast

siegfried
bayreuth festival orchestra
conductor james levine

unpublished radio broadcast

deborah polaski (brünnhilde)
birgitta svenden (erda)
joyce guyer (waldvogel)
wolfgang schmidt (siegfried)
john tomlinson (wanderer)
manfred jung (mime)
ekkehard wlaschiha (alberich)
eric halfvarson (fafner)

384/**31 july 1994**
bayerischer rundfunk broadcast

götterdämmerung
bayreuth festival orchestra and chorus
conductor james levine
chorus-master norbert balatsch

unpublished radio broadcast

deborah polaski (brünnhilde)
anna linden (gutrune)
hanna schwarz (waltraute)
wolfgang schmidt (siegfried)
falk struckmann (gunther)
eric halfvarson (hagen)
ekkehard wlaschiha (alberich)
birgitta svenden (1.norn)
violeta urmana (2.norn)
frances ginzer (3.norn)
joyce guyer (woglinde)
sarah fryer (wellgunde)
jane turner (flosshilde)

385/**1 august 1994**
bayerischer rundfunk broadcast

tristan und isolde
bayreuth festival orchestra and chorus
conductor daniel barenboim
chorus-master norbert balatsch

unpublished radio broadcast

cast as for entry no. 375

386/**2 august 1994**
bayerischer rundfunk broadcast

der fliegende holländer
bayreuth festival orchestra and chorus
conductor peter schneider
chorus-master norbert balatsch

unpublished radio broadcast

cast as for entry no. 364

387/**august-september 1994**
unitel film sessions without audience

tristan und isolde
bayreuth festival orchestra and chorus
conductor daniel barenboim
chorus-master norbert balatsch

unpublished video recording

cast as for entry no. 375

388/25 july 1995
bayerischer rundfunk broadcast

tannhäuser
bayreuth festival orchestra and chorus
conductor donald runnicles
chorus-master norbert balatsch

unpublished radio broadcast

tina kieberg (elisabeth)
ulla sippola (venus)
heikki siukola (tannhäuser)
eike wilm schulte (wolfram)
hans sotin (landgraf)
richard brunner (walther von der vogelweide)
ekkehard wlaschiha (biterolf)
clemens bieber (heinrich der schreiber)
sandor solyom-nagy (reinmar von zweter)

389/26 july 1995
bayerischer rundfunk broadcast

tristan und isolde
bayreuth festival orchestra and chorus
conductor daniel barenboim
chorus-master norbert balatsch

unpublished radio broadcast

cast as for entry no. 375

390/**27 july 1995**
bayerischer rundfunk broadcast

das rheingold
bayreuth festival orchestra
conductor james levine

cd: private archive vienna

cast as for entry no. 381

391/**28 july 1995**
bayerischer rundfunk broadcast

die walküre
bayreuth festival orchestra
conductor james levine

cd: private archive vienna

cast as for entry no. 382

392/**30 july 1995**
bayerischer rundfunk recording

siegfried
bayreuth festival orchestrra
conductor james levine

cd: private archive vienna

cast as for entry no. 383

393/**1 august 1995**
bayerischer rundfunk broadcast

götterdämmerung
bayreuth festival orchestra and chorus
conductor james levine
chorus-master norbert balatsch

cd: private archive vienna

cast as for entry no. 384

394/**2 august 1995**
bayerischer rundfunk broadcast

parsifal
bayreuth festival orchestra and chorus
conductor giuseppe sinopoli
chorus-master norbert balatsch

unpublished radio broadcast

placido domingo (parsifal)
janis martin (kundry)
bernd weikl (amfortas)
hans sotin (gurnemanz)
matthias hölle (titurel)
franz mazura (klingsor)
andrea bönig (stimme von oben)
christiane hossfeld (1.blumenmädchen)
joyce guyer (2.blumenmädchen)
simone schröder (3.blumenmädchen)
katerina beranova (4.blumenmädchen)
marie-claire o'reirdan (5.blumenmädchen)
jane turner (6.blumenmädchen and 2.knappe)
richard brunner (1.gralsritter)
sandor solyom-nagy (2.gralsritter)
sarah fryer (1.knappe)
helmut pampuch (3.knappe)
peter maus (4.knappe)

395/**25 july 1996**
bayerischer rundfunk recording

die meistersinger von nürnberg
bayreuth festival orchestra
and chorus
conductor daniel barenboim
chorus-master norbert balatsch

unpublished radio broadcast

renée fleming (eva)
birgitta svenden (magdalene)
peter seiffert (stolzing)
endrik wottrich (david)
robert holl (sachs)
eric halfvarson (pogner)
hans-joachim ketelsen (kothner)
andreas schmidt (beckmesser)
bernhard schneider (vogelgesang)
roman trekel (nachtigall)
torsten kerl (zorn)
peter maus (eisslinger)
helmut pampuch (moser)
sandor solyom-nagy (ortel)
alfred reiter (schwarz)
jon pescevich (foltz)
kwangchul youn (nachtwächter)

396/**26 july 1996**
bayerischer rundfunk recording

tristan und isolde
bayreuth festival orchestra
and chorus
conductor daniel barenboim
chorus-master norbert balatsch

cassette tape: house of opera (usa)

waltraud meier (isolde)
uta priew (brangäne)
siegfried jerusalem (tristan acts 1 and 2)
wolfgang schmidt (tristan act 3)
falk struckmann (kurwenal)
matthias hölle (marke)
poul elming (melot)
endrik wottrich (junger seemann)
peter maus (hirt)
sandor solyom-nagy (steuermann)

397/**27 july 1996**
bayerischer rundfunk broadcast

das rheingold
bayreuth festival orchestra
conductor james levine

unpublished radio broadcast

beate bilandzija (freia)
rest of cast as for entry no. 381

398/**28 july 1996**
bayerischer rundfunk broadcast

die walküre
bayreuth festival orchestra
conductor james levine

unpublished radio broadcast

matthias hölle (hunding)
anne schwanewilms (gerhilde)
ulla sippola (waltraute)
andrea bönig (schwertleite)
jane turner (siegrunr)
anne wilkens (rossweisse)
rest of cast as for entry no. 382

399/**30 july 1996**
bayerischer rundfunk broadcast

siegfried
bayreuth festival orchestra
conductor james levine

unpublished radio broadcast

cast as for entry no. 383

400/**1 august 1996**
bayerischer rundfunk broadcast

götterdämmerung
bayreuth festival orchestra
and chorus
conductor james levine
chorus-master norbert balatsch

cd: house of opera (usa)
also issued on cassette tape by house of opera (usa)

anne schwanewilms (gutrune)
ulla sippola (2.norn)
rest of cast as for entry no. 384

401/2 **august 1996**
bayerischer rundfunk broadcast

parsifal
bayreuth festival orchestra and chorus
conductor giuseppe sinopoli
chorus-master norbert balatsch

unpublished radio broadcast

poul elming (parsifal)
john tomlinson (gurnemanz)
günter von kannen (klingsor)
rest of cast as for entry no. 394

402/ **25 july 1997**
bayerischer rundfunk broadcast

tristan und isolde
bayreuth festival orchestra and chorus
conductor daniel barenboim
chorus-master norbert balatsch

unpublished radio broadcast

siegfried jerusalem (tristan)
cast as for entry no. 396

403/ **26 july 1997**
bayerischer rundfunk broadcast

die meistersinger von nürnberg
bayreuth festival orchestra and chorus
conductor daniel barenboim
chorus-master norbert balatsch

unpublished radio broadcast

emily magee (eva)
jyrki korhonen (foltz)
rest of cast as entry for no. 395

404/27 july 1997
bayerischer rundfunk broadcast

das rheingold
bayreuth festival orchestra
conductor james levine

unpublished radio broadcast

hanna schwarz (fricka)
nina stemme (freia)
birgitta svenden (erda)
john tomlinson (wotan)
richard brunner (froh)
siegfried jerusalem (loge)
manfred jung (mime)
ekkehard wlaschiha (alberich)
john wegner (donner)
rené pape (fasolt)
eric halfvarson (fafner)
joyce guyer (woglinde)
sarah fryer (wellgunde)
jane turner (flosshilde)

405/28 july 1997
bayerischer rundfunk broadcast

die walküre
bayreuth festival orchestra
conductor james levine

unpublished radio broadcast

deborah polaski (brünnhilde)
tina kiberg (sieglinde)
hanna schwarz (fricka)
poul elming (siegmund)
hans sotin (hunding)
john tomlinson (wotan)
frances ginzer (helmwige)
yvonne naef (waltraute)
anne schwanewilms (gerhilde)
mary lloyd-davies (ortlinde)
birgitta svenden (grimgerde)
anne wilkens (rossweisse)
andrea bönig (schwertleite)
jane turner (siegrune)

406/**30 july 1997**
bayerischer rundfunk broadcast

siegfried
bayreuth festival orchestra
conductor james levine

unpublished radio broadcast

deborah polaski (brünnhilde)
joyce guyer (waldvogel)
birgitta svenden (erda)
wolfgang schmidt (siegfried)
manfred jung (mime)
john tomlinson (wanderer)
ekkehard walachiha (alberich)
eric halfvarson (fafner)

407/**1 august 1997**
bayerischer rundfunk broadcast

götterdämmerung
bayreuth festival orchestra
and chorus
conductor james levine
chorus-master norbert balatsch

unpublished radio broadcast
according to mike ashman the production of
götterdämmerung was also recorded for
television but remains unpublished

deborah polaski (brünnhilde)
anne schwanewilms (gutrune)
hanna schwarz (waltraute)
wolfgang schmidt (siegfried)
falk struckmann (gunther)
eric halfvarson (hagen)
ekkehard wlaschiha (alberich)
birgitta svenden (1.norn)
yvonne naef (2.norn)
frances ginzer (3.norn)
joyce guyer (woglinde)
sarah fryer (wellgunde)
jane turner (flosshilde)

408/**2 august 1997**
bayerischer rundfunk broadcast

parsifal
bayreuth festival orchestra
and chorus
conductor giuseppe sinopoli
chorus-master norbert balatsch

unpublished radio broadcast

poul elming (parsifal)
janis martin (kundry)
falk struckmann (amfortas)
hans sotin (gurnemanz)
günter von kannen (klingsor)

410/**26 july 1998**
bayerischer rundfunk broadcast

die meistersinger von nürnberg
bayreuth festival orchestra
and chorus
conductor daniel barenboim
chorus-master norbert balatsch

unpublished radio broadcast

peter seiffert (stolzing acts 1 and 2)
robert dean smith (stolzing act 3)
rest of cast as for entry no. 403

409/**25 july 1998**
bayerischer rundfunk broadcast

der fliegende holländer
bayreuth festival orchestra
and chorus
conductor peter schneider
chorus-master norbert balatsch

cd: house of opera (usa)

cheryl studer (senta)
marga schiml (mary)
alan titus (holländer)
hans sotin (daland)
roland wagenführer (erik)
torsten kerl (steuermann)

411/**27 july 1998**
bayerischer rundfunk broadcast

das rheingold
bayreuth festival orchestra
conductor james levine

unpublished radio broadcast

emily magee (freia)
jorma silvasti (loge)
hans-joachim ketelsen (donner)
rest of cast as for entry no. 404

412/**28 july 1998**
bayerischer rundfunk broadcast

die walküre
bayreuth festival orchestra
conductor james levine

unpublished radio broadcast

ingrid haubold (ortlinde)
lioba braun (waltraute)
hans sotin (hunding)
rest of cast as for entry no. 405

413/**30 july 1998**
bayerischer rundfunk broadcast

siegfried
bayreuth festival orchestra
conductor james levine

unpublished radio broadcast

cast as for entry no. 406

414/**1 august 1998**
bayerischer rundfunk broadcast

götterdämmerung
bayreuth festival orchestra and chorus
conductor james levine
chorus-master norbert balatsch

unpublished radio broadcast

eike wilm schulte (gunther)
birgitta svenden (1.norn)
lioba braun (2.norn)
rest of cast as for entry no. 407

415/**2 august 1998**
bayerischer rundfunk recording

parsifal
bayreuth festival orchestra and chorus
conductor giuseppe sinopoli
chorus-master norbert balatsch

unpublished video recording

poul elming (parsifal)
linda watson (kundry)
andreas schmidt (amfortas)
hans sotin (gurnemanz)
matthias hölle (titurel)
ekkehard wlaschiha (klingsor)
andrea bönig (stimme von oben)
claudia barainsky (1.blumenmädchen)
joyce guyer (2.blumenmädchen)
simone schröder (3.blumenmädchen)
katerina beranova (4.blumenmädchen)
dorothee jansen (5.blumenmädchen)
laura nykänen (6.blumenmädchen)
richard brunner (1.gralsritter)
sandor solyom-nagy (2.gralsritter)
sarah fryer (1.knappe)
jane turner (2.knappe)
helmut pampuch (3.knappe)
peter maus (4.knappe)

416/ **august 1998**
unitel film sessions without audience

parsifal
bayreuth festival orchestra and chorus
conductor giuseppe sinopoli
chorus-master norbert balatsch

unpublished video recording

falk struckmann (amfortas)
rest of cast as for entry no. 415

417/**june 1999**
teldec recording sessions without audience

die meistersinger von nürnberg
bayreuth festival orchestra
and chorus
conductor daniel barenboim
chorus-master norbert balatsch

cd: teldec 3984 293332

emily magee (eva)
birgitta svenden (magdalene)
peter seiffert (stolzing)
endrik wottrich (david)
robert holl (sachs)
matthias hölle (pogner)
hans-joachim ketelsen (kothner)
andreas schmidt (beckmesser)
bernhard schneider (vogelgesang)
roman trekel (nachtigall)
torsten kerl (zorn)
peter maus (eisslinger)
sandor solyom-nagy (ortel)
helmut pampuch (moser)
alfred reiter (schwarz)
jyrki korhonen (foltz)
kwangchul youn (nachtwächter)

418/**25 july 1999**
bayerischer rundfunk broadcast

lohengrin
bayreuth festival orchestra
and chorus
conductor antonio pappano
chorus-master norbert balatsch

unpublished radio broadcast

melanie diener (elsa)
gabriele schnaut (ortrud)
roland wagenführer (lohengrin)
jean-philippe lafont (telramund)
john tomlinson (könig heinrich)
roman trekel (heerrufer)
michael howard (1.edler)
arnold bezuyen (2.edler)
attila jun (3.edler)
jyrki korhonen (4.edler)

419/**26 july 1999**
bayerischer rundfunk broadcast

der fliegende holländer
bayreuth festival orchestra and chorus
conductor peter schneider
chorus-master norbert balatsch

cassette tape: house of opera (usa)

cast as for entry no. 409

420/**27 july 1999**
bayerischer rundfunk broadcast

parsifal
bayreuth festival orchestra and chorus
conductor giuseppe sinopoli
chorus-master norbert balatsch

unpublished radio broadcast

poul elming (parsifal)
violeta urmana (kundry)
falk struckmann (amfortas)
hans sotin (gurnemanz)
matthias hölle (titurel)
günter von kannen (klingsor)
simone schröder (stimme von oben, 3.blumenmädchen and 1.knappe)
claudia barainsky (1.blumenmädchen)
kirsten blanck (2.blumenmädchen)
caroline stein (4.blumenmädchen)
dorothee jansen (5.blumenmädchen)
laura nykänen (6.blumenmädchen)
arnold bezuyen (1.gralsritter)
sandor solyom-nagy (2.gralsritter)
jane turner (2.knappe)
helmut pampuch (3.knappe)
peter maus (4.knappe)

421/**28 july 1999**
bayerischer rundfunk broadcast

tristan und isolde
bayreuth festival orchestra
and chorus
conductor daniel barenboim
chorus-master norbert balatsch

unpublished radio broadcast

lioba braun (brangäne)
matthias hölle (marke)
bernhard schneider (junger seemann)
rest of cast as for entry no. 402

422/**29 july 1999**
bayerischer rundfunk broadcast

die meistersinger von nürnberg
bayreuth festival orchestra
and chorus
conductor daniel barenboim
chorus-master norbert balatsch

unpublished radio broadcast

robert dean smith (stolzing)
rest of cast as for entry no. 417

423/**26 july 2000**
bayerischer rundfunk broadcast

das rheingold
bayreuth festival orchestra
conductor giuseppe sinopoli

cd: private edition vienna
cd: house of opera (usa)
*das rheingold also issued by
house of opera (usa) on cassette
tape*

*alan titus (wotan)
birgit remmert (fricka)
ricarda merbeth (freia)
mette ejsing (erda)
hans-joachim ketelsen (donner)
roland wagenführer (froh)
kim begley (loge)
michael howard (mime)
günter von kannen (alberich)
johann tilli (fasolt)
philip kang (fafner)
dorothee jansen (woglinde)
natasha petrinsky (wellgunde)
laura nykänen (flosshilde)*

424/**27 july 2000**
bayerischer rundfunk broadcast

die walküre
bayreuth festival orchestra
conductor giuseppe sinopoli

cd: private edition vienna
cd: house of opera (usa)

*gabriele schnaut (brünnhilde)
waltraud meier (sieglinde)
birgit remmert (fricka)
placido domingo (siegmund)
alan titus (wotan)
philip kang (hunding)
irene theorin (ortlinde)
ricarda merbeth (gerhilde)
judit nemeth (waltraute)
johanna duras (schwertleite)
eva ryden (helmwige)
jane irwin (siegrune)
annette jahns (grimgerde)
yumi koyama (rossweisse)*

425/**29 july 2000**
bayerischer rundfunk broadcast

siegfried
bayreuth festival orchestra
conductor giuseppe sinopoli

cd: private edition vienna

gabriele schnaut (brünnhilde)
claudia barainsky (waldvogel)
mette ejsing (erda)
wolfgang schmidt (siegfried)
alan titus (wanderer)
michael howard (mime)
günter von kannen (alberich)
philip kang (fafner)

426/**31 july 2000**
bayerischer rundfunk broadcast

götterdämmerung
bayreuth festival orchestra
and chorus
conductor giuseppe sinopoli
chorus-master eberhard friedrich

cd: private edition vienna

gabriele schnaut (brünnhilde)
ricarda merbeth (gutrune)
violeta urmana (waltraute)
wolfgang schmidt (siegfried)
hans-joachim ketelsen (gunther)
john tomlinson (hagen)
günter von kannen (alberich)
mette ejsing (1.norn)
irmgard vilsmaier (2.norn)
judit nemeth (3.norn)
dorothee jansen (woglinde)
natasha petrinsky (wellgunde)
laura nykänen (flosshilde)

götterdämmerung also issued on cd by
house of opera (usa)

427/**1 august 2000**
bayerischer rundfunk broadcast

die meistersinger von nürnberg
bayreuth festival orchestra
and chorus
conductor christian thielemann
chorus-master eberhard friedrich

cassette tape: house of opera (usa)

robert dean smith (stolzing)
michelle breedt (magdalene)
arnold bezuyen (moser)
rest of cast as for entry no. 417

428/**2 august 2000**
bayerischer rundfunk broadcast

lohengrin
bayreuth festival orchestra
and chorus
conductor antonio pappano
chorus-master eberhard friedrich

cd: house of opera (usa)

linda watson (ortrud)
rest of cast as for entry no. 418

429/**25 july 2001**
bayerischer rundfunk broadcast

die meistersinger von nürnberg
bayreuth festival orchestra
and chorus
conductor christian thielemann
chorus-master eberhard friedrich

unpublished radio broadcast

emily magee (eva)
michelle breedt (magdalene)
robert dean smith (stolzing)
clemens bieber (david)
robert holl (sachs)
guido jentjens (pogner)
hans-joachim ketelsen (kothner)
andreas schmidt (beckmesser)
bernhard schneider (vogelgesang)
alexander marco-buhrmester (nachtigall)
arnold bezuyen (zorn)
peter maus (eisslinger)
helmut pampuch (moser)
sandor solyom-nagy (ortel)
alfred reiter (schwarz)
jyrki korhonen (foltz)
attila jun (nachtwächter)

430/**26 july 2001**
bayerischer rundfunk broadcast

lohengrin
bayreuth festival orchestra and chorus
conductor antonio pappano
chorus-master eberhard friedrich

cd: house of opera (usa)
also issued by house of opera on cassette tape

melanie diener (elsa)
linda watson (ortrud)
peter seiffert (lohengrin)
oskar hillebrandt (telramund)
stephen west (könig heinrich)
roman trekel (heerrufer)
bernard schneider (1.edler)
arnold bezuyen (2.edler)
attila jun (3.edler)
jyrki korhonen (4.edler)

248

431/27 july 2001
bayerischer rundfunk broadcast

das rheingold
bayreuth festival orchestra
conductor adam fischer
*adam fischer replaced giuseppe
sinopoli as conductor*

unpublished radio broadcast

*endrik wottrich (froh)
graham clark (loge)
rest of cast as for entry no. 423*

432/28 july 2001
bayerischer rundfunk broadcast

die walküre
bayreuth festival orchestra
conductor adam fischer
*adam fischer replaced giuseppe
sinopoli as conductor*

unpublished radio broadcast

*luana devol (brünnhilde)
violeta urmana (sieglinde)
birgit remmert (fricka)
robert dean smith (siegmund)
alan titus (wotan)
philip kang (hunding)
ricarda merbeth (helmwige)
irene theorin (ortlinde)
lioba braun (siegrune)
irmgard vilsmaier (gerhilde)
yumi koyama (rossweisse)
judit nemeth (waltraute)
elena zhidkova (schwertleite)
annette jahns (grimerde)*

433/**30 july 2001**
bayerischer rundfunk broadcast

siegfried
bayreuth festival
conductor adam fischer
adam fischer replaced giuseppe sinopoli as conductor

unpublished radio broadcast

luana devol (brünnhilde)
britta stallmeister (waldvogel)
mette ejsing (erda)
christian franz (siegfried)
alan titus (wanderer)
graham clark (mime)
günter von kannen (alberich)
philip kang (fafner)

434/**1 august 2001**
bayerischer rundfunk broadcast

götterdämmerung
bayreuth festival orchestra and chorus
conductor adam fischer
chorus-master eberhard friedrich
adam fischer replaced giuseppe sinopoli as conductor

unpublished radio broadcast

luana devol (brünnhilde)
lioba braun (waltraute)
rest of cast as for entry no. 426

435/**3 august 2001**
bayerischer rundfunk broadcast

parsifal
bayreuth festival orchestra and chorus
conductor christian thielemann
chorus-master eberhard friedrich

cd: private edition vienna

poul elming (parsifal)
violeta urmana (kundry)
andreas schmidt (amfortas)
matthias hölle (gurnemanz)
alfred reiter (titurel)
hartmut welker (klingsor)
simone schröder (stimme von oben, 3.blumenmädchen and 1.knappe)
britta stallmeister (1.blumenmädchen)
katerina beranova (2.blumenmädchen)
caroline stein (4.blumenmädchen)
dorothee jansen (5.blumenmädchen)
laura nykänen (6.blumenmädchen)
arnold bezuyen (1.gralsritter)
sandor solyom-nagy (2.gralritter)
jane turner (2.knappe)
helmut pampuch (3.knappe)
peter maus (4.knappe)

436/**10 august 2001**
bayerischer rundfunk broadcast of performance marking 125 years of bayreuth festival and 50 years since the 1951 re-opening

beethoven: symphony no 9 "choral"
bayreuth festival orchestra and chorus
conductor christian thielemann
chorus-master eberhard friedrich

cd: private edition vienna

emily magee
michelle breedt
robert dean smith
robert holl

437/**25 july 2002**
bayerischer rundfunk broadcast

tannhäuser
bayreuth festival orchestra and chorus
conductor christian thielemann
chorus-master eberhard friedrich

cd: private edition vienna
this edition is incorrectly dated 26 july

ricarda merbeth (elisabeth)
barbara schneider-hofstetter (venus)
glenn winslade (tannhäuser)
roman trekel (wolfram)
kwangchul youn (landgraf)
clemens bieber (walther von der vogelweide)
john wegner (biterolf)
arnold bezuyen (heinrich der schreiber)
alexander marco-buhrmester (reinmar von zweter)
eugenia grekova (ein junger hirt)

438/**26 july 2002**
bayerischer rundfunk broadcast

lohengrin
bayreuth festival orchestra and chorus
conductor andrew davis
chorus-master eberhard friedrich

unpublished radio broadcast

petra maria schnitzer (elsa)
linda watson (ortrud)
peter seiffert (lohengrin)
jean-philippe lafont (telramund)
roman trekel (heerrufer)
bernhard schneider (1.edler)
arnold bezuyen (2.edler)
attila jun (3.edler)
hans griepentrog (4.edler)

439/**27 july 2002**
bayerischer rundfunk broadcast

das rheingold
bayreuth festival orchestra
conductor adam fischer

unpublished radio broadcast

alan titus (wotan)
mihoko fujimara (fricka)
anja kampe (freia)
simone schröder (erda)
olaf bär (donner)
endrik wottrich (froh)
grahan clark (loge)
michael howard (mime)
hartmut welker (alberich)
johann tilli (fasolt)
philip kang (fafner)
caroline stein (woglinde)
natasha petrinsky (wellgunde)
elena zhidkova (flosshilde)

440/**28 july 2002**
bayerischer rundfunk broadcast

die walküre
bayreuth festival orchestra
conductor adam fischer

unpublished radio broadcast

evelyn herlitzius (brünnhilde)
violeta urmana (sieglinde)
mihoko fujimara (fricka)
alan titus (wotan)
robert dean smith (siegmund)
philip kang (hunding)
irene theorin (helmwige)
anja kampe (gerhilde)
yvonne wiedstruck (ortlinde)
daniela sindram (siegrune)
yumi koyama (rossweisse)
judit nemeth (waltraute)
elena zhidkova (schwertleite)
simone schröder (grimgerde)

441/30 july 2002
bayerischer rundfunk broadcast

siegfried
bayreuth festival orchestra
conductor adam fischer

unpublished radio broadcast

evelyn herlitzius (brünnhilde)
eugenia grekova (waldvogel)
simone schröder (erda)
christian franz (siegfried)
alan titus (wanderer)
graham clark (mime)
hartmut welker (alberich)
philip kang (fafner)

442/1 august 2002
bayerischer rundfunk broadcast

götterdämmerung
bayreuth festival orchestra
and chorus
conductor adam fischer
chorus-master eberhard friedrich

unpublished radio broadcast

evelyn herlitzius (brünnhilde)
yvonne wiedstruck (gutrune)
lioba braun (waltraute)
wolfgang schmidt (siegfried)
olaf bär (gunther)
john tomlinson (hagen)
hartmut welker (alberich)
simone schröder (1.norn)
irmgard vilsmaier (2.norn)
judit nemeth (3.norn)
caroline stein (woglinde)
natasha petrinsky (wellgunde)
elena zhidkova (flosshilde)

443/2 august 2002
bayerischer rundfunk broadcast

die meistersinger von nürnberg
bayreuth festival orchestra and chorus
conductor christian thielemann
chorus-master eberhard friedrich

cd: private edition vienna

alexander marco-buhrmester (kothner)
klaus häger (nachtigall)
hans griepentrog (schwarz)
jörg simon (foltz)
rest of cast as for entry no. 429

444/25 july 2003
bayerischer rundfunk broadcast

der fliegende holländer
bayreuth festival orchestra and chorus
conductor marc albrecht
chorus-master eberhard friedrich

adrienne dugger (senta)
uta priew (mary)
john tomlinson (holländer)
jaakko ryhänen (daland)
endrik wottrich (erik)
tomislav muzek (steuermann)

445/26 july 2003
bayerischer rundfunk broadcast

tannhäuser
bayreuth festival orchestra and chorus
conductor christian thielemann
chotus-master eberhard friedrich

cd: private edition vienna

robin johannsen (ein junger hirt)
rest of cast as for entry no. 437

446/27 july 2003
bayerischer rundfunk broadcast

das rheingold
bayreuth festival orchestra
conductor adam fischer

unpublished radio broadcast

arnold bezuyen (loge)
daniela sindram (wellgunde)
rest of cast as for entry no. 439

447/28 july 2003
bayerischer rundfunk broadcast

die walküre
bayreuth festival orchestra
conductor adam fischer

unpublished radio broadcast

cast as for entry no. 440

448/30 july 2003
bayerischer rundfunk broadcast

siegfried
bayreuth festival orchestra
conductor adam fischer

unpublished radio broadcast

eva schneider (waldvogel)
rest of cast as for entry no. 441

449/1 august 2003
bayerischer rundfunk broadcast

götterdämmerung
bayreuth festival orchestra
and chorus
conductor adam fischer
chorus-master eberhard friedrich

unpublished radio broadcast

christian franz (siegfried)
peter klaveness (hagen)
daniela sindram (wellgunde)
rest of cast as entry for no. 442

450/2 august 2003
bayerischer rundfunk broadcast

lohengrin
bayreuth festival orchestra and chorus
conductor andrew davis
chorus-master eberhard friedrich

unpublished radio broadcast

petra-maria schnitzer (elsa)
judit nemeth (ortrud)
peter seiffert (lohengrin)
john wegner (telramund)
reinhard hagen (könig heinrich)
tomislav muzek (1.edler)
helmut pampuch (2.edler)
attila jun (3.edler)
alexander marco-buhrmester (4.edler)

451/25 july 2004
bayerischer rundfunk broadcast

parsifal
bayreuth festival orchestra and chorus
conductor pierre boulez
chorus-master eberhard friedrich

cd: private edition vienna

endrik wottrich (parsifal)
michelle de young (kundry)
alexander marco-buhrmester (amfortas)
robert holl (gurnemanz)
kwangchul youn (titurel)
john wegner (klingsor)
simone schröder (stimme von oben)
julia borchert (1.blumenmädchen and 1.knappe)
martina rüping (2.blumenmadchen)
carola guber (3.blumenmädchen)
anna korondi (4.blumenmädchen)
jutta maria böhnert (5.blumenmädchen)
atala schöck (6.blumenmädchen and 2.knappe)
tomislav muzek (1.gralsritter)
samuel youn (2.gralsritter)
norbert ernst (3.knappe)
miljenko turk (4.knappe)

452/**26 july 2004**
bayerischer rundfunk broadcast

tannhäuser
bayreuth festival orchestra and chorus
conductor christian thielemann
chorus-master eberhard friedrich

cd: private edition vienna

stephen gould (tannhäuser)
ricarda merbeth (elisabeth)
judit nemeth (venus)
roman trekel (wolfram)
kwangchul youn (landgraf)
clemens bieber (walther von der vogelweide)
john wegner (biterolf)
arnold bezuyen (heinrich der schreiber)
alexander marco-buhrmester (reinmar von zweter)
robin johannsen (ein junger hirt)

453/27 july 2004
bayerischer rundfunk broadcast

das rheingold
bayreuth festival orchestra
conductor adam fischer

unpublished radio broadcast

alan titus (wotan)
mihoko fujimara (fricka)
anja kampe (freia)
simone schröder (erda)
olaf bär (donner)
endrik wottrich (froh)
arnold bezuyen (loge)
michael howard (mime)
hartmut welker (alberich)
johann tilli (fasolt)
philip kang (fafner)
caroline stein (woglinde)
daniela sindram (wellgunde)
sarah castle (flosshilde)

454/28 july 2004
bayerischer rundfunk broadcast

die walküre
bayreuth festival orchestra
conductor adam fischer

unpublished radio broadcast

evelyn herlitzius (brünnhilde)
eva johansson (sieglinde)
mihoko fujimara (fricka)
alan titus (wotan)
robert dean smith (siegmund)
philip kang (hunding)
anja kampe (gerhilde)
yvonne wiedstruck (ortlinde)
irmgard vilsmaier (waltraute)
simone schröder (schwertleite)
irene theorin (helmwige)
daniela sindram (siegrune)
sarah castle (grimgerde)
yumi koyama (rossweisse)

455/30 july 2004
bayerischer rundfunk broadcast

siegfried
bayreuth festival orchestra
conductor adam fischer

unpublished radio broadcast

evelyn herlitzius (brünnhilde)
robin johannsen (waldvogel)
simone schröder (erda)
christian franz (siegfried)
alan titus (wanderer)
graham clark (mime)
hartmut welker (alberich)

456/1 august 2004
bayerischer rundfunk broadcast

götterdämmerung
bayreuth festival orchestra
and chorus
conductor adam fischer
chorus-master eberhard friedrich

unpublished radio broadcast

evelyn herlitzius (brünnhilde)
yvonne wiedstruck (gutrune)
mihoko fujimara (waltraute)
christian franz (siegfried)
olaf bär (gunther)
peter klaveness (hagen)
hartmut welker (alberich)
simone schröder (1.norn)
irmgard vilsmaier (2.norn)
judit nemeth (3.norn)
caroline stein (woglinde)
daniela sindram (wellgunde)
sarah castle (flosshilde)

457/**25 july 2005**
bayerischer rundfunk broadcast

tristan und isolde
bayreuth festival orchestra and chorus
conductor eiji oue
chorus-master eberhard friedrich

unpublished radio broadcast

nina stemme (isolde)
petra lang (brangäne)
robert dean smith (tristan)
andreas schmidt (kurwenal)
kwangchul youn (marke)
alexander marco-buhrmester (melot)
clemens bieber (ein junger seemann)
arnold bezuyen (hirt)
martin snell (steuermann)

458/**26 july 2005**
bayerischer rundfunk broadcast

lohengrin
bayreuth festival orchestra and chorus
conductor peter schneider
chorus-master eberhard friedrich

unpublished radio broadcast

linda watson (ortrud)
arnold bezuyen (1.edler)
miljenko turk (3.edler)
martin snell (4.edler)
rest of cast as for entry no. 450

459/**27 july 2005**
bayerischer rundfunk broadcast

der fliegende holländer
bayreuth festival orchestra and chorus
conductor marc albrecht
chorus-master eberhard friedrich

unpublished radio broadcast

norbert ernst (steuermann)
rest of cast as for entry no. 444

460/**28 july 2005**
bayerischer rundfunk broadcast

tannhäuser
bayreuth festival orchestra and chorus
conductor christian thielemann
chorus-master eberhard friedrich

unpublished radio broadcast

guido jentjens (landgraf)
rest of cast as for entry no. 452

461/**29 july 2005**
bayerischer rundfunk broadcast

parsifal
bayreuth festival orchestra and chorus
conductor pierre boulez
chorus-master eberhard friedrich

unpublished radio broadcast

alfons eberz (parsifal)
clemens bieber (1.knappe)
rest of cast as for entry no. 451

462/22 august 2005/bayreuth oberfrankenhalle
bayerischer rundfunk recording of a special concert commemorating cosima, siegfried and winifred wagner

cd: private edition vienna

der fliegende holländer overture
bayreuth festival orchestra
conductor marc albrecht

siegfried wagner: das flüchlein das jeder mitbekam, overture
bayreuth festival orchestra
conductor peter schneider

wesendonk-lieder
bayreuth festival orchestra
conductor pierre boulez

ricarda merbeth

lohengrin act three prelude and treulich geführt (brautchor)
bayreuth festival orchestra and chorus
conductor peter schneider
chorus-master eberhard friedrich

tannhäuser overture
bayreuth festival orchestra
conductor christian thielemann

liszt: a faust symphony, alles vergängliche (schlusschor)
bayreuth festival orchestra and chorus
conductor christian thielemann
chorus-master eberhard friedrich

arnold bezuyen

463/**26 july 2006**
bayerischer rundfunk broadcast

das rheingold
bayreuth festival orchestra
conductor christian thielemann

unpublished radio broadcast

michelle breedt (fricka)
satu vihavainen (freia)
mihoko fujimara (erda)
falk struckmann (wotan)
ralf lukas (donner)
clemens bieber (froh)
arnold bezuyen (loge)
gerhard siegel (mime)
andrew shore (alberich)
kwangchul youn (fasolt)
jyrki korhonen (fafner)
fionnula mccarthy (woglinde)
ulrike hetzel (wellgunde)
marina prudenskaja (flosshilde)

464/**27 july 2006**
bayerischer rundfunk broadcast

die walküre
bayreuth festival orchestra
conductor christian thielemann

unpublished radio broadcast

linda watson (brünnhilde)
adianne pieczonska (sieglinde)
michelle breedt (fricka)
falk struckmann (wotan)
endrik wottrich (siegmund)
kwangchul youn (hunding)
satu vihavainen (gerhilde)
amanda mace (ortlinde)
martine dike (waltraute)
janet collins (schwertleite)
irene théorin (helmwige)
wilke te bummelstroete (siegrune)
annette küttenbaum (grimgerde)
alexandra petersamer (rossweisse)

dates and casts for these 2006 performances taken from advance information and therefore subject to change

465/**29 july 2006**
bayerischer rundfunk broadcast

siegfried
bayreuth festival orchestra
conductor christian thielemann

unpublished radio broadcast

linda watson (brünnhilde)
robin johannsen (waldvogel)
mihoko fujimara (erda)
stephen gould (siegfried)
gerhard siegel (mime)
falk struckmann (wanderer)
andrew shore (alberich)
jyrki korhonen (fafner)

466/**31 july 2006**
bayerischer rundfunk broadcast

götterdämmerung
bayreuth festival orchestra
and chorus
conductor christian thielemann
chorus-master eberhard friedrich

unpublished radio broadcast

linda watson (brünnhilde)
gabriele fontana (gutrune)
mihoko fujimara (waltraute)
stephen gould (siegfried)
alexander marco-buhrmester (gunther)
hans-peter könig (hagen)
andrew shore (alberich)
janet collins (1.norn)
martine dike (2.norn)
irene théorin (3.norn)
fionnula mccarthy (woglinde)
ulrike hetzel (wellgunde)
marina prudenskaja (flosshilde)

dates and casts for these 2006 performances taken from advance information and therefore subject to change

appendix a/ **index of works**
reference numbers are the session numbers, not page numbers
*indicates abridged recording/ +indicates filmed version

der fliegende holländer
complete recordings

025	070	075	083	084	109	115	123	129
165	193	207	214	256	265	274	284	290
303	317	319+	350	364	372	377	386	409
419	444	459						

excerpts

019	108	348	462

tannhäuser
complete recordings

006*	059a	076	122	133	139	152	163	167
183	215	228	230	250	258	263+	311	321
331	344	345+	367	376	388	437	445	452
460								

excerpts

001	108	462

lohengrin
complete recordings

048	065	100	110	116	132	140	177	186
216	264	275	285	292	293+	328	339	349+
351	378	418	428	430	438	450	458	

excerpts

014	015	016	018	108	347	462

tristan und isolde
complete recordings

005*	023	041	054	091	098	103	113	131
145	151	166	173	175+	188	196	201	229
237	248	282	289	300	302+	320	330	375
385	387+	389	396	402	421	457		

excerpts

007

index of works/continued
die meistersinger von nürnberg
complete recordings

010	*027*	*028*	*029*	*036*	*047*	*082*	*089*	*092*
099	*101*	*111*	*114*	*130*	*144*	*153*	*185*	*195*
202	*222*	*231*	*238*	*283*	*291*	*295*	*309*	*310+*
327	*332*	*395*	*403*	*410*	*417*	*422*	*427*	*429*
443								

excerpts

108	*150+*	*243*	*347*

das rheingold
complete recordings

032	*037*	*043*	*050*	*055*	*061*	*071*	*077*	*085*
094	*104*	*117*	*125*	*135*	*146*	*155*	*159*	*169*
178	*189*	*196*	*203*	*210*	*217*	*224*	*232*	*239*
244	*252*	*259*	*267*	*276*	*280+*	*296*	*305*	*313*
322	*334*	*340*	*352*	*357+*	*360*	*368*	*381*	*390*
397	*404*	*411*	*423*	*431*	*439*	*446*	*453*	*463*

excerpts

001	*004*

die walküre
complete recordings

024	*033*	*038*	*044*	*051*	*056*	*062*	*069*	*072*
078	*086*	*095*	*105*	*118*	*126*	*136*	*147*	*156*
160	*170*	*176+*	*179*	*184*	*190*	*197*	*204*	*211*
218	*225*	*233*	*240*	*245*	*253*	*260*	*268*	*271+*
277	*297*	*306*	*314*	*323*	*335*	*341*	*353*	*361*
365+	*369*	*382*	*391*	*398*	*405*	*412*	*424*	*432*
440	*447*	*454*	*464*					

excerpts

001	*004*	*016*	*019*	*020*

siegfried
complete recordings

013	*034*	*039*	*045*	*052*	*057*	*063*	*073*	*079*
087	*096*	*106*	*119*	*127*	*137*	*148*	*157*	*161*
171	*180*	*191*	*198*	*205*	*212*	*219*	*226*	*234*
241	*246*	*254*	*261*	*269*	*272+*	*278*	*298*	*307*
315	*324*	*336*	*342*	*354*	*362*	*366+*	*370*	*383*
392	*399*	*406*	*413*	*425*	*433*	*441*	*448*	*455*
465								

excerpts

001	*004*	*015*	*017*

index of works/concluded
götterdämmerung
complete recordings

021	026	035	040	046	053	059	064	074
080	088	097	107	120	128	138	149	158
162	172	181	192	199	206	213	220	227
235	242	247	255	262	270	279	281+	299
308	316	326	337	343	355	358+	363	371
384	393	400	407+	414	426	434	442	449
456	466							

excerpts

001	011	108

parsifal
complete recordings

008	031	042	049	068	081	090	093	102
112	121	124	134	141	143	154	164	168
182	187	194	200	208	221	223	236	249
251	257	266	273	286	287+	288	301	304
312	318	329	333	338	356	359	373	374
379	380	394	401	408	415	416+	420	435
451	461							

excerpts

002	022	108	348

siegfried idyll

294	348

wesendonk-lieder
462

beethoven: symphony no 9 "choral"

009	030	058	066	067	142	436

works by other composers

001	294	325	462

*appendix b/***index of conductors**
reference numbers are the session numbers, not page numbers
*indicates that only excerpts were recorded

abendroth	meistersinger
m.albrecht	holländer
barenboim	tristan/meistersinger/ring/parsifal
böhm	holländer/tristan/meistersinger/ring/beethoven ninth
boulez	tristan/ring/parsifal
cluytens	tannhäuser/lohengrin/meistersinger/parsifal
a.davis	lohengrin
c.davis	tannhäuser
elder	meistersinger
elmendorff	tannhäuser/tristan/meistersinger/walküre/siegfried/götterdämmerung
erede	lohengrin
a.fischer	ring
furtwängler	lohengrin*/tristan*/meistersinger/walküre*/götterdämmerung/beethoven ninth
hindemith	beethoven ninth
hoesslin	ring*/parsifal*
hollreiser	tannhäuser/meistersinger
jochum	lohengrin/tristan/parsifal
karajan	tristan/meistersinger/ring
keilberth	holländer/tannhäuser/lohengrin/ring
kempe	lohengrin/ring
c.kleiber	tristan
klobucar	tannhäuser/meistersinger/ring
knappertsbusch	holländer/meistersinger/ring/parsifal
kraus	holländer
krauss	ring/parsifal
krips	meistersinger
leinsdorf	tannhäuser/meistersinger
levine	ring/parsifal
maazel	lohengrin/ring
matacic	lohengrin
melles	tannhäuser
muck	parsifal*

index of conductors/concluded

nelsson	holländer/lohengrin
oue	tristan
pappano	lohengrin
pitz	holländer*/tannhäuser*/lohengrin*/meistersinger*/ götterdämmerung*/parsifal*
runnicles	tannhäuser
russell davies	holländer
sabata	tristan
sawallisch	holländer/tannhäuser/lohengrin/tristan
schippers	meistersinger/walküre
schneider	holländer/lohengrin/ring
schonwandt	meistersinger
sinopoli	holländer/tannhäuser/lohengrin/ring/parsifal
solti	ring
stein	meistersinger/ring/parsifal
strauss	parsifal/beethoven ninth
suitner	holländer/tannhäuser/walküre/siegfried/götterdämmerung
thielemann	tannhäuser/meistersinger/ring/parsifal/beethoven ninth
tietjen	holländer*/lohengrin*/walküre/siegfried*
varviso	holländer/lohengrin/meistersinger
waart	lohengrin
s.wagner	parsifal*
wallat	meistersinger

Discographies by Travis & Emery:

Discographies by John Hunt.

1987: From Adam to Webern: the Recordings of von Karajan.
1991: 3 Italian Conductors and 7 Viennese Sopranos: 10 Discographies: Arturo Toscanini, Guido Cantelli, Carlo Maria Giulini, Elisabeth Schwarzkopf, Irmgard Seefried, Elisabeth Gruemmer, Sena Jurinac, Hilde Gueden, Lisa Della Casa, Rita Streich.
1992: Mid-Century Conductors and More Viennese Singers: 10 Discographies: Karl Boehm, Victor De Sabata, Hans Knappertsbusch, Tullio Serafin, Clemens Krauss, Anton Dermota, Leonie Rysanek, Eberhard Waechter, Maria Reining, Erich Kunz.
1993: More 20th Century Conductors: 7 Discographies: Eugen Jochum, Ferenc Fricsay, Carl Schuricht, Felix Weingartner, Josef Krips, Otto Klemperer, Erich Kleiber.
1994: Giants of the Keyboard: 6 Discographies: Wilhelm Kempff, Walter Gieseking, Edwin Fischer, Clara Haskil, Wilhelm Backhaus, Artur Schnabel.
1994: Six Wagnerian Sopranos: 6 Discographies: Frieda Leider, Kirsten Flagstad, Astrid Varnay, Martha Moedl, Birgit Nilsson, Gwyneth Jones.
1995: Musical Knights: 6 Discographies: Henry Wood, Thomas Beecham, Adrian Boult, John Barbirolli, Reginald Goodall, Malcolm Sargent.
1995: A Notable Quartet: 4 Discographies: Gundula Janowitz, Christa Ludwig, Nicolai Gedda, Dietrich Fischer-Dieskau.
1996: The Post-War German Tradition: 5 Discographies: Rudolf Kempe, Joseph Keilberth, Wolfgang Sawallisch, Rafael Kubelik, Andre Cluytens.
1996: Teachers and Pupils: 7 Discographies: Elisabeth Schwarzkopf, Maria Ivoguen, Maria Cebotari, Meta Seinemeyer, Ljuba Welitsch, Rita Streich, Erna Berger.
1996: Tenors in a Lyric Tradition: 3 Discographies: Peter Anders, Walther Ludwig, Fritz Wunderlich.
1997: The Lyric Baritone: 5 Discographies: Hans Reinmar, Gerhard Hüsch, Josef Metternich, Hermann Uhde, Eberhard Wächter.
1997: Hungarians in Exile: 3 Discographies: Fritz Reiner, Antal Dorati, George Szell.
1997: The Art of the Diva: 3 Discographies: Claudia Muzio, Maria Callas, Magda Olivero.
1997: Metropolitan Sopranos: 4 Discographies: Rosa Ponselle, Eleanor Steber, Zinka Milanov, Leontyne Price.
1997: Back From The Shadows: 4 Discographies: Willem Mengelberg, Dimitri Mitropoulos, Hermann Abendroth, Eduard Van Beinum.
1997: More Musical Knights: 4 Discographies: Hamilton Harty, Charles Mackerras, Simon Rattle, John Pritchard.
1998: Conductors On The Yellow Label: 8 Discographies: Fritz Lehmann, Ferdinand Leitner, Ferenc Fricsay, Eugen Jochum, Leopold Ludwig, Artur Rother, Franz Konwitschny, Igor Markevitch.
1998: More Giants of the Keyboard: 5 Discographies: Claudio Arrau, Gyorgy Cziffra, Vladimir Horowitz, Dinu Lipatti, Artur Rubinstein.

1998: Mezzos and Contraltos: 5 Discographies: Janet Baker, Margarete Klose, Kathleen Ferrier, Giulietta Simionato, Elisabeth Höngen.
1999: The Furtwängler Sound Sixth Edition: Discography and Concert Listing.
1999: The Great Dictators: 3 Discographies: Evgeny Mravinsky, Artur Rodzinski, Sergiu Celibidache.
1999: Sviatoslav Richter: Pianist of the Century: Discography.
2000: Philharmonic Autocrat 1: Discography of: Herbert Von Karajan [Third Edition].
2000: Wiener Philharmoniker 1 - Vienna Philharmonic & Vienna State Opera Orchestras: Disc. Part 1 1905-1954.
2000: Wiener Philharmoniker 2 - Vienna Philharmonic & Vienna State Opera Orchestras: Disc. Part 2 1954-1989.
2001: Gramophone Stalwarts: 3 Separate Discographies: Bruno Walter, Erich Leinsdorf, Georg Solti.
2001: Singers of the Third Reich: 5 Discographies: Helge Roswaenge, Tiana Lemnitz, Franz Völker, Maria Müller, Max Lorenz.
2001: Philharmonic Autocrat 2: Concert Register of Herbert Von Karajan Second Edition.
2002: Sächsische Staatskapelle Dresden: Complete Discography.
2002: Carlo Maria Giulini: Discography and Concert Register.
2002: Pianists For The Connoisseur: 6 Discographies: Arturo Benedetti Michelangeli, Alfred Cortot, Alexis Weissenberg, Clifford Curzon, Solomon, Elly Ney.
2003: Singers on the Yellow Label: 7 Discographies: Maria Stader, Elfriede Trötschel, Annelies Kupper, Wolfgang Windgassen, Ernst Häfliger, Josef Greindl, Kim Borg.
2003: A Gallic Trio: 3 Discographies: Charles Münch, Paul Paray, Pierre Monteux.
2004: Antal Dorati 1906-1988: Discography and Concert Register.
2004: Columbia 33CX Label Discography.
2004: Great Violinists: 3 Discographies: David Oistrakh, Wolfgang Schneiderhan, Arthur Grumiaux.
2006: Leopold Stokowski: Second Edition of the Discography.
2006: Wagner Im Festspielhaus: Discography of the Bayreuth Festival.
2006: Her Master's Voice: Concert Register and Discography of Dame Elisabeth Schwarzkopf [Third Edition].
2007: Hans Knappertsbusch: Kna: Concert Register and Discography of Hans Knappertsbusch, 1888-1965. Second Edition.
2008: Philips Minigroove: Second Extended Version of the European Discography.
2009: American Classics: The Discographies of Leonard Bernstein and Eugene Ormandy.

Discography by Stephen J. Pettitt, edited by John Hunt:
1987: Philharmonia Orchestra: Complete Discography 1945-1987

Available from: Travis & Emery at 17 Cecil Court, London, UK. (+44) 20 7 240 2129. email on sales@travis-and-emery.com .

© Travis & Emery 2009

Music and Books published by Travis & Emery Music Bookshop:

Anon.: Hymnarium Sarisburense, cum Rubris et Notis Musicus
Agricola, Johann Friedrich from Tosi: Anleitung zur Singkunst. (Faksimile 1757)
Bach, C.P.E.: edited W. Emery: Nekrolog or Obituary Notice of J.S. Bach.
Bateson, Naomi Judith: Alcock of Salisbury
Bathe, William: A Briefe Introduction to the Skill of Song
Bax, Arnold: Symphony #5, Arranged for Piano Four Hands by Walter Emery
Burney, Charles: The Present State of Music in France and Italy
Burney, Charles: The Present State of Music in Germany, The Netherlands …
Burney, Charles: An Account of the Musical Performances … Handel
Burney, Karl: Nachricht von Georg Friedrich Handel's Lebensumstanden.
Burns, Robert (jnr): The Caledonian Musical Museum (1810 volume)
Cobbett, W.W.: Cobbett's Cyclopedic Survey of Chamber Music. (2 vols.)
Corrette, Michel: Le Maitre de Clavecin
Crimp, Bryan: Dear Mr. Rosenthal … Dear Mr. Gaisberg …
Crimp, Bryan: Solo: The Biography of Solomon
d'Indy, Vincent: Beethoven: Biographie Critique
d'Indy, Vincent: Beethoven: A Critical Biography
d'Indy, Vincent: César Franck (in French)
Fischhof, Joseph: Versuch einer Geschichte des Clavierbaues
Frescobaldi, Girolamo: D'Arie Musicali per Cantarsi. Primo Libro & Secondo Libro.
Geminiani, Francesco: The Art of Playing the Violin.
Handel; Purcell; Boyce; Green et al: Calliope or English Harmony: Volume First.
Hawkins, John: A General History of the Science and Practice of Music (5 vols.)
Herbert-Caesari, Edgar: The Science and Sensations of Vocal Tone
Herbert-Caesari, Edgar: Vocal Truth
Hopkins and Rimboult: The Organ. Its History and Construction.
Hunt, John: some 40 discographies – see list of discographies
Isaacs, Lewis: Hänsel and Gretel. A Guide to Humperdinck's Opera.
Isaacs, Lewis: Königskinder (Royal Children) A Guide to Humperdinck's Opera.
Lacassagne, M. l'Abbé Joseph : Traité Général des élémens du Chant.
Lascelles (née Catley), Anne: The Life of Miss Anne Catley.
Mainwaring, John: Memoirs of the Life of the Late George Frederic Handel
Malcolm, Alexander: A Treaty of Music: Speculative, Practical and Historical
Marx, Adolph Bernhard: Die Kunst des Gesanges, Theoretisch-Practisch
May, Florence: The Life of Brahms
Mellers, Wilfrid: Angels of the Night: Popular Female Singers of Our Time
Mellers, Wilfrid: Bach and the Dance of God

Travis & Emery Music Bookshop
17 Cecil Court, London, WC2N 4EZ, United Kingdom.
Tel. (+44) 20 7240 2129

Music and Books published by Travis & Emery Music Bookshop:

Mellers, Wilfrid: Beethoven and the Voice of God
Mellers, Wilfrid: Caliban Reborn - Renewal in Twentieth Century Music
Mellers, Wilfrid: François Couperin and the French Classical Tradition
Mellers, Wilfrid: Harmonious Meeting
Mellers, Wilfrid: Le Jardin Retrouvé, The Music of Frederic Mompou
Mellers, Wilfrid: Music and Society, England and the European Tradition
Mellers, Wilfrid: Music in a New Found Land: …… American Music
Mellers, Wilfrid: Romanticism and the Twentieth Century (from 1800)
Mellers, Wilfrid: The Masks of Orpheus: …… the Story of European Music.
Mellers, Wilfrid: The Sonata Principle (from c. 1750)
Mellers, Wilfrid: Vaughan Williams and the Vision of Albion
Panchianio, Cattuffio: Rutzvanscad Il Giovine.
Pearce, Charles: Sims Reeves, Fifty Years of Music in England.
Pettitt, Stephen: Philharmonia Orchestra: Complete Discography 1945-1987
Playford, John: An Introduction to the Skill of Musick.
Purcell, Henry et al: Harmonia Sacra … The First Book, (1726)
Purcell, Henry et al: Harmonia Sacra … Book II (1726)
Quantz, Johann: Versuch einer Anweisung die Flöte traversiere zu spielen.
Rameau, Jean-Philippe: Code de Musique Pratique, ou Methodes.
Rastall, Richard: The Notation of Western Music.
Rimbault, Edward: The Pianoforte, Its Origins, Progress, and Construction.
Rousseau, Jean Jacques: Dictionnaire de Musique
Rubinstein, Anton : Guide to the proper use of the Pianoforte Pedals.
Sainsbury, John S.: Dictionary of Musicians. Vol. 1. (1825). 2 vols.
Simpson, Christopher: A Compendium of Practical Musick in Five Parts
Spohr, Louis: Autobiography
Spohr, Louis: Grand Violin School
Tans'ur, William: A New Musical Grammar; or The Harmonical Spectator
Terry, Charles Sanford: Four-Part Chorals of J.S. Bach. (German & English)
Terry, Charles Sanford: Joh. Seb. Bach, Cantata Texts, Sacred and Secular.
Terry, Charles Sanford: The Origins of the Family of Bach Musicians.
Tosi, Pierfrancesco: Opinioni de' Cantori Antichi, e Moderni
Van der Straeten, Edmund: History of the Violoncello, The Viol da Gamba …
Van der Straeten, Edmund: History of the Violin, Its Ancestors… (2 vols.)
Walther, J. G.: Musicalisches Lexikon ober Musicalische Bibliothec (1732)

Travis & Emery Music Bookshop
17 Cecil Court, London, WC2N 4EZ, United Kingdom.
Tel. (+44) 20 7240 2129

© Travis & Emery 2009

www.ingramcontent.com/pod-product-compliance
Lightning Source LLC
Chambersburg PA
CBHW071833230426
43671CB00012B/1947